The Partnering Imperative

Making business partnerships work

Anne Deering

Anne Murphy

JOHN WILEY & SONS, LTD

Other Wiley Editorial Offices

John Wiley & Sons Inc., 111 River Street, Hoboken, NJ 07030, USA

Jossey-Bass, 989 Market Street, San Francisco, CA 94103-1741, USA

Wiley-VCH Verlag GmbH, Boschstr. 12, D-69469 Weinheim, Germany

John Wiley & Sons Australia Ltd, 33 Park Road, Milton, Queensland 4064, Australia

John Wiley & Sons (Asia) Pte Ltd, 2 Clementi Loop #02-01, Jin Xing Distripark, Singapore 129809

John Wiley & Sons Canada Ltd, 22 Worcester Road, Etobicoke, Ontario, Canada M9W 1L1

Library of Congress Cataloging-in-Publication Data

Deering, Anne, 1959-
   The partnering imperative: making business partnerships work / by Anne Deering and
Anne Murphy.
      p. cm.
   Includes bibliographical references and index.
   ISBN 0–470–85159–7 (alk. paper)
      1. Strategic alliances (Business) 2. Business networks. 3. Joint ventures. I. Murphy,
Anne, 1955- II. Title.

HD69.S8D44 2003
658′.044–dc21

                                                                                2003041120

British Library Cataloguing in Publication Data

A catalogue record for this book is available from the British Library

ISBN 0 470 85159 7

Typeset Kolam Information Services Private Limited, Pondicherry, India
Printed and bound in Great Britain by Biddles Ltd, Guildford and King's Lynn.
This book is printed on acid-free paper responsibly manufactured from sustainable forestry in which at
least two trees are planted for each one used for paper production.

To our children, Eva, Tanya, Elena, Alexander, Samuel, Benjamin and Sophie. May you grow up in a world of collaboration and tolerance

Contents

List of Figures and Tables

Figures

Table

Boxes

Acknowledgements

Writing this book has been an act of creative partnership. Our debt of gratitude extends over a wide community of writers and thinkers too numerous to mention individually, who have taken the trouble to set down their thoughts and share them and who have helped to shape our thinking over the years.

For their unstinting generosity in sharing their research and for inspiring us with their energy in the search for new ways of seeing, we thank Chris Blantern, Max Boisot, Tom Boydell, Robert Dilts, Charles Hampden-Turner, Bob Lewis, Julian Russell and Rose Trevelyan.

Our thanks also to the many members of the original research consortium for sharing with us their partnering experiences and insights.

For their openness and the spirit of learning with which they shared their corporate stories, we thank Sir Robin Saxby of ARM, Malcolm Johnson of SEEBOARD and Jose Mari Larrañaga of Mondragón Corporación Cooperativa.

For their trust, in the early days of the research and for sticking with us as we took the first steps towards the philosophy presented in this book, we thank Mike Ash-Edwards, Simon Carter, Peter Cromer, John Higgins, Paul Joachim, Myriam Kamhi, David Keltie, Sally Randall, Graham Stevenson and Karen Winder. (There are others we would like to thank whom we cannot name, without jeopardizing the anonymity of some of the case material.)

To Jenny Athanasiadou for her outstanding graphics; to Gregory Thomas and Anindya Mukherjee for their creative and compelling research; to Sally Davies for her 'detective' work; to Fritz Kroeger, Nancy Bishop and Graeme Deans for their energy and ideas in reviewing the manuscript; to Tara Clouse for her patience and commitment to managing the process; and to our friends at Wiley, Claire Plimmer and Jo Golesworthy – thank you to a great team.

As always, love and thanks to Tanyia Brown for her care and support which gave the space and opportunity to write (and the nagging to get on with it!).

Most especially, our thanks to Tom Lloyd, for his extraordinary patience and expertise.

To our husbands, Angus and Fernando, for their support and encouragement in the precarious balancing act of combining work and home, our love and gratitude.

Introduction

Wishing me with him, partner of his fortune
Shakespeare, *Two Gentlemen of Verona*

Until a few years ago the large, integrated organization was the undisputed king of the business world. Now its crown is being contested by groups of organizations operating in concert. The intensity of competition is not abating, quite the contrary, but the nature of business rivalry is changing. Co-operation is ceasing to be the opposite of competition and is becoming, instead, one of its preferred instruments.

It is no longer a controversial idea that the main competitive agent in the future will not be integration but networks of autonomous companies with complementary skills and resources pursuing shared objectives. Even those who remain convinced that the best way to assemble a particular set of resources, or to achieve a desired market position, is to acquire other companies, are quite ready to outsource non-core functions to sub-contractors or partners. 'Partnering', as we shall call all forms of inter-firm co-operation, including joint ventures and so-called 'strategic alliances', has become an increasingly important theme. Even in industries such as telecommunications, pharmaceuticals and auto making, where the urge to acquire or merge appears still to dominate strategic thinking, partnering is playing an increasingly critical role.

As the network-owning segment of the global telecommunications industry was being drastically re-shaped by acquisitions at the turn of the century, for example, the carriers' strategic thinkers were all coming to the conclusion that the only way to prepare their firms for the age of 'wireless data' (in which mobile phones become internet access devices) was to forge 'strategic alliances' with internet service and 'portal' companies, content providers, software developers and 'smartphone' manufacturers. They saw acquisition as appropriate when strengthening their physical networks, but saw partnering as a better way to establish strong positions in mobile data, where network ownership confers no significant advantage.

The internet is acting as a crucial catalyst in what, looking back, will be seen as a historic shift in the emphasis of strategy from acquisitions to partnering, for two main reasons. The first is that the internet is itself a complex, rapidly growing partnership, in which power and information will always be widely distributed. This is not only making partnering preferable to acquisition, in what Harvard Business School's Jeffrey Rayport calls the 'marketspace' itself; it is also infecting strategic thinking elsewhere, in the traditional 'marketplace' with its embedded partnering philosophy.

Second, acquisitions are permanent commitments and companies are beginning to realize that it is unwise to make permanent commitments in fast-changing environments. Here, too, the 'marketspace' is changing the 'marketplace' as the rhythms of traditional business accelerate and approach internet speed.

As we will see in Chapter 1, it is now generally recognized that partnering is a vital business development mechanism and a powerful value creator, but the secrets of successful partnering remain elusive.

Partnering works in theory, but far too many alliances, initially billed as bold, resource-leveraging plays, have foundered on conflicts of interest or clashes of personalities or have absorbed huge amounts of management time – for very little return. Because partnerships can end for reasons other than failure, it is hard to assess the partnership failure rate, but a reasonable guess is that barely one in three partnerships works, in the sense that they meet their objectives and earn a return in excess of their cost of capital.

It is for this reason that acquisition, in spite of its attendant financial and cultural risks, is still seen by many business managers as the 'safest' way to secure and retain the additional resources, competences and markets that their increasingly 'global' strategies demand. After a lull in M&A activity in the early to mid-1990s, there was a sharp acceleration of M&A activity, as companies in turbulent industries such as telecommunications, pharmaceuticals, banking, publishing and entertainment, aggressively jockeyed for position. After the bursting of the 'dotcom' bubble and the disappearance of high-priced equity (the favourite acquisition currency during the 1995–2001 merger wave), M&A activity abated, but no one believes this is more than a lull. M&A remains the default strategy for ambitious CEOs.

Although all the evidence suggests that most acquisitions destroy value for the acquirers' shareholders, hope continues to triumph over experience. Something, after all, has to be done when industries are colliding, new entrants are pouring out of the woodwork and predators are on the rampage.

Some acquisitions work and the takeover system still has an important role to play in the consolidation of established industries and as a discipline that keeps managers on their toes. It is unlikely, however, that the stock market will continue to accept without question such a demonstrably problematic strategy. As we shall see in Chapter 1, partnering can present a much better strategic option than acquisition. We believe companies that persist with acquisition strategies because they are easier to implement, more 'fashionable' or more impressive demonstrations of a CEO's prerogative will be at a competitive disadvantage to companies that persevere with partnering and learn how to make it work. (See Appendix A for thoughts on which approach might work best for you.)

As a corporate stratagem, however, partnering remains vague and ill defined and, despite all the literature that has appeared on the subject in recent years, its management implications are not well understood. Company leaders must understand that, although partnerships deliver benefits comparable, in some ways, to those promised by acquisitions, partnering is a fundamentally different approach to combining resources. Partnerships live between firms, rather than within them, are more in the mind than on the balance sheet and are much harder to implement than acquisitions. They challenge conventional strategic wisdoms, require new forms of communication and new approaches to management and oblige partnering practitioners to learn a new language.

In this book we explain why partnering is a better option than acquiring in today's business environment, explore the implications for managers of the variations on the partnering theme and describe (and explain how to use) a simple but powerful tool for diagnosing partnering problems and maximizing partnership performance.

Business partnerships tend not to be evident to casual observers because partners rarely believe it is in their interests to make them so. As we shall see in Chapter 1, however, partnering has grown so rapidly over the past 15 years or so that it is reasonable to talk of the end of the era of 'integrated' enterprise and of the beginning of a new era of 'partnership' enterprise. We will identify the forces that are fuelling the partnering trend, explain how 'globalization' and technological convergence oblige organizations of all kinds to seek partners among 'alien' (in both a business and an ethnic sense) cultures and review the management literature on the subject. We will challenge the belief that harmony is essential in a partnership by suggesting that the real value of partnerships lies in the differences between the partners and that any efforts to eradicate them will, therefore, destroy value.

In Chapter 2 we will describe the findings of our research into partnerships, which was designed to develop a new management language for partnering. We will introduce the main product of the research, the 'partnering grid' and illustrate its use with a case study. The grid is a 2×3 matrix, correlating ambition on one axis with perceptions of difference on the other. Many who have used it say it is the best language they have come across for discussing partnering and partnership perceptions.

Chapter 3 will explain how the grid can be used to find compatible partners and how it can illuminate the patterns of power in partnerships by helping partners to understand one another better. Those who have used the grid have found its power to reveal how individual partners feel about themselves and their roles in a partnership particularly valuable.

In Chapter 4 we will show why the key challenge in partnership enterprise is to find ways to live profitably with the unavoidable differences between partners. We will explain that by seeking out and then acting on 'common ground', partners can reap mutual benefits in spite of their differences.

We will argue, in Chapter 5, that the search for common ground by different partners leads to emergent, rather than intentional strategies and we will suggest that, since structure is an important aspect of strategy, structure too must be emergent. We conclude the chapter with a description of a high-technology company that has demonstrated the power of emergent strategy and structure in turbulent business environments.

In Chapter 6 we will describe the kinds of 'conversation' partners need to engage in to reach the common ground from which joint action can 'emerge'. We will suggest that mutually beneficial strategies and structures are more likely to emerge if partners develop the habits and abide by the principles of what we call 'working dialogue'.

In Chapter 7 we will examine the nature of leadership in enterprises where power and knowledge are widely distributed. We will refer to leadership in scientific research groups as an analogy for the knowledge-based and innovation-seeking partnerships we believe will come to dominate business over the next decade. We will suggest that the key role of leaders in fluid enterprises with emergent strategies and structures is to develop and maintain a system of containment that provides just enough, but no more than just enough, security to realize the creative potential of the coming together of complementary differences.

In the final chapter we will summarize our position by re-stating the case against partnering in the language we have derived from the grid and by showing that it is based on deeply flawed conceptions of the roles of trust and conflict in modern business relationships.

We conclude many of the eight chapters with a 'story from the front'. We have not attempted to interpret or to apply these stories directly to the preceding text or to direct the reader to the 'important points'. We hope the connections are clear, but we are also sure that you will make your own applications and interpretations in ways we could not possibly predict. Make of the stories what you will. We have found all of them illuminating in one way or another and hope you will also.

The partnering grid plays an important role in this book and we want to make sure it is used as well as understood. We have therefore included in Appendix B a diagnostic tool that allows you to do a first mapping of your own situation to the grid. In Appendix C we offer you a series of questions to help you define the context of your partnership and check the fit of your partnering style to that context.

A final word about relationship: there has been much discussion about task versus relationship in theory about management, seeking to segregate one from the other and to indicate situations in which one has primacy over the other.[1] Reality, however, has a different story to tell. We believe that both are critical to success in any business context but in partnerships more than anywhere else. Without relationship, task cannot be delivered successfully; without task, the relationship has no purpose. In the words of Margaret Wheatley, 'in the quantum world, relationships are not just interesting...they are all there is to reality'.[2]

References

1. *The Managerial Grid: Key Orientations for Achieving Production through People*, Robert R. Blake and Jane S. Mouton (Gulf Publishing, 1964); *Management of Organizational Behavior: Leading Human Resources* (8th edn), Paul Hersey, Kenneth H. Blanchard and Dewey E. Johnson (Prentice Hall, 2000); *A Theory of Leadership Effectiveness*, Fred E. Fiedler (McGraw-Hill, 1967).
2. *Leadership and the New Science*, Margaret Wheatley (Berrett-Koehler, 1999).

1

A new kind of enterprise

*You pays your money and you takes
your choice*

Punch, 1846

First the good news: there is a business strategy that can bring you 25%
greater share value than that of your competitors. And now for the bad
news: 70% of companies can't make this strategy work.

The strategy, of course, is partnering. The ability to create value through
the skilful management of portfolios of business partnerships is an important
source of competitive advantage. We maintain that it is one of the essen-
tials of business success in the new millennium.

The trend reflects, not a sudden outbreak of corporate gregariousness, but
a belief that, in today's fast-changing and ever more complex environment,
companies must look beyond their own corporate boundaries and seek to
create win–win relationships with other companies who provide complementary capabilities.

Constantly accelerating change in the business environment is all we can
be certain of these days: this premise is now so widely accepted it has
become a cliché. Some say the era of rapid, unpredictable change has
been ignited by the growing intensity of global competition. Others see it
as an inevitable consequence of technological convergence. Some are
anxious about it. Others welcome it as a source of new opportunities for
the agile and the alert.

However it is explained and perceived, the reality for practically everyone in
this era of accelerating change is working with a bewildering, rapidly prolifer-
ating array of different possibilities, cultures, visions, agendas, opportunities

and threats. But there's no agreement about what to do. While we are being bombarded by the obvious fact of change, we are being deafened by a cacophony of different and frequently conflicting views about what it means and what its management implications are.

It is not just business either. The whole world seems beset by conflict and contradiction. Even established democracies are struggling to cope with the problems of youth violence, social fragmentation and ethnic isolation. Our faith in the old dream of integration and harmony is fading. We may wish it were not so, but we have to learn to live with the consequences.

Despite the constant, heroic attempts to reach across the old divisions and forge new partnerships to solve pressing social and economic problems, the divisions persist and the bridge builders and mediators are looked at, for the most part, with cynicism and apathy. People appear, if not content with all their difference and disagreements, at least under no great pressure to resolve or settle them.

While many company leaders still dream of integration and harmony, shifting market boundaries, growing customer choice, increased stakeholder pressure, the communications revolution and, above all, the resurgence of the high-speed, high-tech, high-risk and totally unpredictable e-business world are making the business of business much too complex for old, monocultural organizations to cope with on their own.

Large organizations are having to face the fact that the bureaucracies with which they once ruled their markets cannot handle the seething multitude of different and often conflicting voices, creeds, philosophies and agendas of modern business. The control their bureaucracies were designed to exert is slipping from their grasp, because the systems in their charge are becoming too complex and unpredictable.

There are two conflicting points of view on how organizations might respond to the loss of control, both of which are in action within the business community. The first is that the problem lies not with bureaucracy and control systems per se, but with their lack of sophistication. According to this view, the complexification of the environment has indeed outstripped the competence of existing control systems, but this is a technical problem – control can and will be reasserted, with the help of modern technology and a few minor modifications to the system. Control is desirable; the only problem is how to re-apply it.

The other, newer perspective questions whether 'control', in the old sense, even if it could be re-applied (which is doubtful) any longer serves a useful purpose. This is such an alarming idea that it is rarely articulated in business and management debates, but it is hard not to see a tacit acceptance of it in the speed at which companies are forming partnerships. For, in adopting partnering strategies, firms are acknowledging that, in practice if not yet in theory, the need for control is less pressing than the need to create or extend networks of business relationships.

The flight from control

There are rich rewards for those who can make partnering work. A.T. Kearney research demonstrates that those companies that display excellence in partnering increasingly out-perform their peers in the stock market.[1] Companies with a history of successful partnership can derive 25 % greater increase in share value relative to the industry sector in which they operate. This performance differential has risen as high as 40 % over the last decade (see Figure 1.1).

But the downside is also significant for those who fail. Our research also tracked the share price impact of companies announcing partnerships and subsequent partnership success or failure. Using a sample of

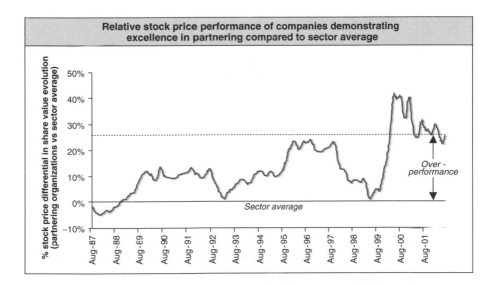

Figure 1.1 *The value of partnering excellence*
Source: A.T. Kearney research and analysis; Datastream data

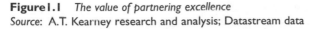

'mega-alliances', those with a value greater than $500m, we tracked the evolution in market value of the companies involved both on announce-ment of an alliance and six months on. The growth in share value of companies participating in alliances that had shown some success at the six-month point showed on average a 5.3 % advantage relative to their industry sector. But those companies operating alliances that could not demonstrate any tangible benefit six months after announcement under-performed the share value growth of their sector by 11.7 % (see Figure 1.2).

Despite the risks involved, there is significant evidence that partnering is on the increase. Studies published by Booz Allen and Andersen Consulting in the 1990s[2] revealed a sharp increase in joint ventures, licensing agree-ments, collaborative research, technology exchanges and marketing alli-ances over the previous decade. US firms formed only 750 such partnerships in the 1970s, but by the mid-90s were forming thousands each year. The growth of alliances accelerated sharply in the second half of the 1990s and, by 1999, 82 % of executives surveyed expected alliances to be a prime

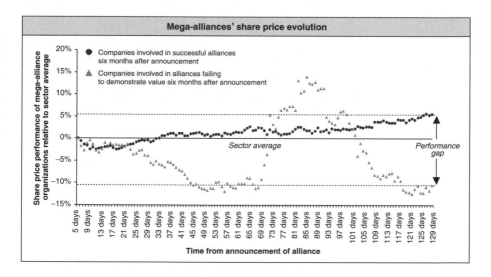

Figure 1.2 *The prize for success – and the price of failure*
Note: The peak at 85 days' post-announcement in the data of alliances failing to demonstrate value at the six month point is driven by the impact of dramatic share price increase of a biotech firm and its pharmaceutical partner against expectations of a therapeutic break-through. Results declined on news of poor drug trial results and questions regarding the pharmaceutical company's marketing skills.
Source: A.T. Kearney research and analysis; Datastream data

growth vehicle in the future. Analysis showed that, by 1999, alliances accounted for 26 % of the average Fortune 500 company's revenues, up from 11 % in 1994 and for 6 to 15 % of the market value of the typical Fortune 500 company.

Bankers were particularly zealous converts to the partnering philosophy and expected their companies to hold average portfolios of over 50 alliances by 2002, accounting for as much as 50 % of revenue.

These results were broadly confirmed by a 2002 Conference Board study which found that, on average, US executives expected alliances to account for 30 % of their revenues by 2004 and that European executives expected the figure to be nearer 40 %.[3]

But the risks remain considerable. The Andersen survey suggested that about 70 % of alliances fail and although the 15 most successful alliances created an estimated $72bn of shareholder value, the 15 least successful destroyed $43bn worth of shareholder value.

Alliance management

Whether or not you agree with the conclusion that the explosion in partnering since the mid-1980s amounts to 'a new chapter in the evolution of free enterprise',[2] it clearly poses new management challenges.

Networks of autonomous systems are far more complex, and less easily guided, than integrated enterprises. In an age when the shelf-life of knowledge can be shorter than the time it takes to capture, let alone make sense of it, they cannot be guided by a deliberate strategy-formulation process. A completely new kind of guidance system is required to handle the uncontrollability and complexity of partnership enterprise and the speed with which decisions now have to be taken.

The problem is that, in abandoning a system in which integrated enterprises managed their environments, firms come face to face with contradiction and paradox. How can they work with different cultures, experiences and values, while yet retaining their sense of self? How can they reconcile their commitment to their principles with the need to adapt their management styles and ways of doing business to each local context? How can they empower partners and other 'stakeholders' (including their own employees) to grasp opportunities without causing chaos? How can they share without risking exploitation or be open to influence without compromising their principles? How can a firm achieve planned change when it lacks full control of its business? How can partners share 'visions' when they see things differently and see different things?

So far, most firms have ignored these dilemmas and treated partnerships in much the same way as acquisitions. They have partnered to strengthen their defences and concentrated on ensuring their partners are the right size and shape to be bricks in their battlements. They have failed to recognize that each brick dreams of being a castle in its own right and the essence of the partnering structure is not the bricks but the mortar which both separates and unites them.

Some have argued that to confine the partnering model to a purely defensive deployment is to deny its true potential and significance. Joseph Badaracco[4] describes the autocratic management style of post-war US companies as a creature of the medieval 'Citadel Paradigm' which must now be replaced by what he calls the 'City-State Paradigm' of Renaissance Italy:

> Against the broad sweep of the history of commerce and business organization, companies as citadels – clearly defined zones of ownership and control, surrounded by market relations – are the anomaly.

Others have predicted that partnering will emerge as the dominant strategic model in rapidly changing environments. Catherine Alter and Jerald Hage[5] argue that 'multi-lateral arrangements, among diverse organizations that band together to produce a single product', are emerging as a major new form of enterprise, because they adapt much more quickly and creatively to changing technologies and markets.

So business leaders have a choice – apply traditional management principles to the new partnership enterprises and risk disintegration or find ways to collaborate without control and risk chaos. Given the complexity of modern business environments, however, the fading of old frontiers between markets and industries, the emergence of the virtual 'marketspace' where partnering is endemic and the incessant struggle for competitive advantage, there is really no choice at all, because very soon 'going it alone' will cease even to be an option.

For all sorts of reasons, to do with technology, competition, politics and access to resources, it is becoming imperative in more and more industries to seek new knowledge and capability through partnering. It is the only way to operate in the marketspace; it is fast becoming the best way to operate in an increasingly competitive and liberal marketplace, and it is the only way to detect and respond quickly enough to the wishes of increasingly diverse and capricious customers.

We will demonstrate in the next chapter, however, that this surrender of control is not necessarily a flight to chaos and destruction. Systems can be under control when no one is in control. The point is illustrated by the surprising similarities between the choice faced by air traffic controllers, as they try to add capacity to over-crowded air corridors, and the choice companies have to make between acquisition and partnership.

At present, air traffic controllers manage one segment of airspace each and 'hold the picture', by mentally adding vectors to their radar screens, with data on speed, headings and rates of descent or climb gathered by communications, navigation and surveillance (CNS) systems.

The only way to add to this system's capacity is to slice the air corridors into ever smaller segments. But because human controllers can only handle a limited number of aircraft at once, and spend a lot of their time managing the handovers into and out of their own sectors, this strategy is subject to diminishing returns and is now close to its limits on the busiest routes (hence the increase in delays and so-called 'stacking').

Everyone recognizes that the solution to the problem is to get computers to 'hold the picture' and have the controllers and pilots manage by exception. Computers can process data much more quickly than human beings can and thus reduce the 'separation' between aircraft deemed to be 'safe' closer to the physical limits imposed by an aircraft's wake and inertia.

There are two possible architectures for a computerized ATC system: ground-based central processing (a computerized version of the present system) or airborne, distributed processing, where aircraft get CNS feeds, communicate with each other and organize their own separation. This system is known as 'free flight' and airlines like the idea because it would be cheaper than a ground-based centralized system and would give them more flexibility and more control over their own costs.

Free flight is alarming for regulators, however, because safety is and must always be their paramount concern and it seems to fly in the face of basic prudence to abandon their central control and put the safety of passengers in the hands of some alleged, self-organizing process that emerges from the interactions of self-guided aircraft. Tests and simulations have shown that free flight works, but a major, psychological barrier stands between it and widespread acceptance, both by the travel industry and the politicians who will ultimately have to sanction it.

The same fear of losing control stands between the partnering strategy and its widespread acceptance as the 'first choice' strategy for assembling the skills and resources needed to enter new markets. Since the evidence shows most acquisitions destroy value for acquirers' shareholders, acquisition must be seen as very risky, but it is not hard to see why, at the time a choice has to be made, it often seems to those making the choice to be much 'safer' than partnering.

But sometimes there is no choice.

Partnering purposes

The inspirations of partnerships are legion, but the strategic drivers that frame and inform the decision to partner can be classified under six main headings.

Technology

Partnerships were a common arrangement for exploiting new technologies long before James Watt and Matthew Boulton joined forces in the 18th century to develop and market Watt's separate condenser steam engine.

In modern times similar partnerships between innovative small companies and large companies strong in marketing and channels were being advocated as alternatives to licensing agreements at the height of the microelectronic revolution in the mid-1970s (Hlavacek et al.)[6] and a decade later, such David and Goliath partnerships were being proclaimed as a good way for small, high-tech firms to establish themselves abroad (Berlew).[7]

The way in which technological advance erodes traditional industry barriers also provides a powerful partnering impetus. AT&T, Motorola, Philips, Sony, Apple and Matsushita, for example, buried the competitive hatchet to become co-investors in General Magic, a small software firm that had established a lead in so-called 'personal intelligent communication' systems (Yoshino and Rangan).[8] Similar relationships are common in the modern pharmaceutical industry, where small firms lead in the development of gene therapies.

Strategy

Although the exchange of skills and resources and the desire for access to distant markets remain important inspirations, the case for partnering has since become much wider.

It has been promoted as a suitable response to periodic plate shifts in the world economy, such as the dissolution of the Soviet bloc, the integration of Europe, the opening up of China, the internet revolution, the globalization of markets, the convergence of consumer needs (Ohmae)[9] and as a useful tool for corporate re-structuring. In one variation on the last theme, a company sells a minority stake in a non-core business and forms a temporary partnership with the buyer by promising to sell the rest later. This allows a buyer to get to know the business it is buying more intimately than would otherwise be possible before paying the full price and offers a seller the chance to add value to the rest of its equity by ensuring a smooth, jointly managed transfer of control (Nanda and Williamson).[10]

Value chain optimization

Another theme of modern partnering is the idea that if traditional, market-based relationships between suppliers and buyers were transformed into more intimate alliances, both parties could benefit.

The idea was first promoted as a way to control a value chain that avoided the problems associated with vertical integration. It was cheaper and less risky, it was argued, to partner with, rather than buy, suppliers and, moreover, much could be learned from distributors about the needs of customers (Narus and Anderson).[11]

The argument was later generalized into a prescription to form value-adding partnerships (VAPs), groups of independent firms that collaborate to manage flows of goods or services along value chains. Johnston and Lawrence[12] described how McKesson, a US distributor of drugs, healthcare products and other consumer goods, was driven to develop a VAP by the business the major drugstore chains were taking from the independent stores McKesson served.

Some saw the interest in value and supply chain management as a recognition of the merits of the Japanese keiretsu (business society) system (Ferguson).[13] Others suggested western firms had already gone beyond the keiretsu and developed a new form of enterprise in which groups of companies (linked together in umbrella networks, through different kinds of alliance, ranging from formal joint ventures, to loose, informal collaborations) coalesce and compete with each other.[5,14]

Politics

Political institutions and government agencies sometimes act as sponsors or catalysts of business partnerships. Japan's Ministry of International Trade & Industry (MITI) was an active sponsor of the successful attacks of Japanese companies on several major world markets over the past two decades and the European Commission was a promoter of both the Prometheus and GSM standard-setting projects.

Some have even argued that national and regional governments can and should sponsor partnerships between local companies, to 'organize' competition and thereby avoid suicidal head-to-head confrontations in world markets (Urban and Vendemini).[15] The 1996 agreement between Japanese and European microchip makers to 'organize' world trade in semiconductors was billed as a private sector initiative. It was known, however, that the European Commission and MITI approved of and helped arrange the meetings of representatives of NEC and Toshiba of Japan, Siemens of Germany and the Franco-Italian group, SGS-Thomson, that agreed the pact.

Setting standards

Partnering is also being increasingly used by groups of competing companies to establish or promote technical standards, such as the VHS video standard and Europe's GSM digital mobile phone system.

The commercialization of the internet is producing scores of such alliances and special interest groups. In wireless data (accessing online sources of data, such as the internet, through a mobile phone), Ericsson, Matsushita, Motorola, Nokia and UK handheld computer company, Psion, formed the Symbian partnership to promote Psion's EPOC operating system. In 1998, Ericsson, IBM, Intel, Nokia and Toshiba formed the 'Bluetooth' special interest group to promote a specification for cheap wireless communications and networking between PCs, mobile phones and other portable devices and later recruited 3Com, Lucent, Microsoft and Motorola, plus over 1,000 smaller firms, to the Bluetooth cause.

The e-partnering imperative

Although there has been a handful of major acquisitions within the internet and e-commerce sector, there have been literally thousands of partnerships, joint ventures and other kinds of alliance. Indeed, it is fair to say that, by the beginning of the year 2000, partnering had firmly established itself as the dominant strategy for growth and market development in e-business.

There are several reasons for this. First, e-business is a far higher speed business than conventional business and partnerships can be formed far more quickly than acquisitions can be completed. Second, speed is vital in e-business, because Metcalfe's 'law of networks', which says the value of a network varies according to the square of its size, gives first movers a huge competitive advantage. Third, because the e-business environment is more volatile and much less predictable than that of conventional business, inter-firm e-business collaborations must be more provisional. Acquisitions lock companies into relationships. Partnerships are intrinsically temporary and can be abandoned much more easily when they cease to be beneficial. (You may find the checklist at Appendix A useful in stimulating discussion around which strategy best suits your circumstances).

Conventional prescriptions

It is one thing to be convinced of the merits of a partnering strategy and quite another to realize its full potential. For although the prospect of outstanding results from synergy and co-creation may be the inspiration for many partnerships, the experience is, all too often, of defensive behaviour and scepticism, leading to conflict and failure. Research by A. T. Kearney suggests that 50 % of strategic alliances and as many as 80 % of supply chain partnerships fail to add value.

It is not clear, either from the literature or from the graveyard of failed alliances, why the mortality rate is so high. Explanations vary, the critics disagree, injured parties lick their wounds in private and sceptics see the failures as evidence that the whole idea of partnering is flawed. Without a proven model for diagnosing partnership failures, observers have had to put them down to ill-defined objectives or cultural conflicts.

There is no shortage of advice as to what can and should be done to improve partnerships. Numerous books and articles have been published with lists of principles for identifying and remedying partnership ailments.[16,17,18,19,20] The experts have emphasized the importance of compatible values and visions, co-operative management styles, knowledge sharing and trust. This is all in tune with the perceptions and experiences of many involved in successful partnerships, but it is hard to disentangle cause and effect – to decide whether partners that apply these principles do so because they happen to get on or whether they get on because they have applied the principles.

Experts assume good principles produce good practice but they cannot prove it and it is often hard to escape the suspicion that the prescriptions stem more from the widespread belief that all organizational problems must have organizational solutions than objective observation. The prescriptions are essentially technical. Relationship issues are treated as problems to which there are generally applicable solutions. There is so much of this kind of advice about, and it is being applied with such enthusiasm, that it is easy to forget it all assumes the relationship is good in the first place.

It is important to choose partners carefully, of course, but trust cannot be guaranteed; it may or may not develop. Most partnering 'gurus' assume ideal relationships as a starting point for their prescriptions that are in most cases impossible to aspire to, let alone achieve. If all they can say when two or more very different corporate cultures come together to pursue joint objectives is that conflict is bad and harmony is good, they can say little that is of much practical use to most real partnerships.

Partnership enterprise

The new model of partnership enterprise that is emerging in the e-world and in some conventional industries too is very different from the conventional multi-unit enterprise and requires a different set of operating principles.

Managers realize that the old, integrated structure, with its hierarchy and functional silos, must be replaced by flatter, process-based architectures, extending beyond their corporate boundaries. But the new architectures have a style requirement. They demand a loosening of control systems, within and between firms, and this has brought issues of understanding and perception to the fore which are more complex and more subtle than the issues managers of the 'old school' are used to dealing with.

The problems companies encounter in partnering are special cases of general management problems associated with relationships within as well as between organizations. Even organizations that have shunned the partnering strategy must confront the effects of downsizing on employer–employee contracts, the dilemmas associated with the desire to empower people, while continuing to control them, and the perceived need to formulate grand visions and develop winning strategies at a time when today's assumptions are so often belied by tomorrow's events.

Managers accept the need for new enterprise forms, with flat, or horizontal shapes, but there is as yet little understanding of the implications of the new architectures for management systems and styles. Enterprise shapes have consequences for management philosophies. You cannot change one without the other. Much that is sensible and valuable has emerged in the literature in recent years about the need for 'empowerment' and the role of leaders. But most of it is based on an outdated philosophy of management that misses the central point about organizations and enterprises: that they must continue to operate effectively, despite the fact that opinions about how things are and what should be done will always differ.

Even if harmony were useful in business relationships, it is not available these days and there is good reason to believe that attempts to achieve it can be harmful. The search for harmony to reduce conflict and promote trust in relationships is the wrong solution to the wrong problem, because if we insist on seeing all partnering problems in terms of trust and conflict, we must accept that they can never be resolved. We will have more to say about trust and conflict at the end of this book. That is where they belong. They are epiphenomena – consequences, not causes.

Trust, although to be hoped for, cannot be an expected precursor to partnering in a world in which prediction of any kind is, at best, superfluous and often downright dangerous.

References

1. A.T. Kearney research and analysis; Datastream data. 20 companies from five industry sectors were tracked over a 15-year time series and share price evolution compared on a smoothed 50-trading day moving average stock price to the average of their sector. Companies' partnering excellence was assessed against

four primary criteria: a history and high frequency of partnerships; relative implementation success sustained over time; a demonstrated partnering culture and belief that partnerships are integral to their strategy; operational benefit derived from partnerships.

2. A practical guide to alliances (Booz Allen & Hamilton, 1995); Maria Gonzalez, *Ivey Business Journal* 47, Volume 66, Issue 1.
3. Howard Muson, *Across the Board* 18, Volume 39, Issue 2.
4. *The Knowledge Link: How Firms Compete Through Strategic Alliances*, J. Badaracco (Harvard Business School Press, 1993).
5. *Organizations Working Together*, C. Alter and J. Hage (Sage, 1993).
6. Tie small business technology to marketing power, J. Hlavacek, B. Dovey et al., *HBR* Jan/Feb, 1977.
7. The joint venture – a way into foreign markets, K. Berlew, *HBR* Jul/Aug, 1984.
8. *Strategic Alliances: An Entrepreneurial Approach to Globalization*, M. Yoshino and S. Rangan (Harvard Business School Press, 1995).
9. The global logic of strategic alliances, K. Ohmae, *HBR* Mar/Apr, 1989.
10. Use joint ventures to ease the pain of restructuring, A. Nanda and P. Williamson, *HBR* Nov/Dec, 1995.
11. Turn your industrial distributors into partners, J. Narus and J. Anderson, *HBR* Mar/Apr, 1986.
12. Beyond vertical integration – the rise of the value-adding partnership, R. Johnston and P. Lawrence, *HBR* Jul/Aug, 1988.
13. Computers and the coming of the U.S. Keiretsu, C. Ferguson, *HBR* Jul/Aug, 1990.
14. Group versus group: how alliance networks compete, B. Gomes-Casseres, *HBR* Jul/Aug, 1994.
15. *European Strategic Alliances: Co-operative Strategies in the New Europe*, S. Urban and S. Vendemini (Blackwell, 1992).
16. Collaborate with your competitors, and Win, G. Hamel, Y. Doz and C. K. Prahalad, *HBR* Jan/Feb, 1989.
17. Collaborative advantage: the art of alliances, R. Moss Kanter, *HBR* Jul/Aug, 1994.
18. *Beyond Negotiation. Redeeming Customer–Supplier Relationships*, J. Carlisle and R. Parker (John Wiley, 1989).
19. *Breakthrough Partnering: Creating a Collective Enterprise Advantage*, P. Moody (Oliver Wight, 1994).
20. Cooperate to compete globally, H. Perlmutter and D. Heenan, *HBR* Mar/Apr, 1986.

2

A new language for partnering

When progress is looking for a partner, it doesn't turn to those who believe they are only average. It turns instead to those who are for ever searching and striving to become the best they possibly can
A. Lou Vickery, *How to be a Winner: The Athlete's Notebook*

While there is no shortage of strategic reasons for taking partnering seriously, there is certainly a dearth of credible explanations as to why so many fail. The failure rates for any form of corporate relationship are becoming so predictably high as to be rendered meaningless. Like the rising divorce statistics, they have become an uncomfortable reality against which many see no option but to gamble with the future.

There is, however, another way of seeing and understanding partnerships, a way that is not such a game of chance. To play, however, our cherished assumption about what makes corporate relationships work needs to be squarely challenged: the assumption that harmony and sameness are both means and end.

The consistent theme in the literature surrounding the failure phenomenon is to suggest that culture, or more specifically cultural difference, is the root cause of defeat. Too often anything seen as intangible, understood as invisible, and tacitly agreed as undiscussable, is placed in this cultural coverall. Parked in the backwater of 'soft' issues, it receives little further focused attention.

This has left us in the untenable position of knowing that to add real value in a globalizing economy we must be able to form productive corporate relationships with organizations that are different from us; and we must do this armed only with the advice that such relationships only work when we choose organizations that are pretty well the same in the first place.

Faced with universally abysmal success rates, many organizations understandably follow contemporary advice and manage these differences by trying to get rid of them. Such a strategy is the most expensive option of all as it both erodes the value of creative potential and eats up resource in perpetual alignment activities and risk management. Companies must manage both risk and opportunity with equal passion and equal agility and they will not do this by playing the cultural safe hand of sameness.

All enterprises need partnerships now and, given their complexity, volatility and diversity, it is impractical to seek such ideal relationships. Companies must recognize the intrinsic imperfectability of their relationships. They must devote less time and energy to harmonizing and aligning and more to *understanding* their partners and using this understanding to find their 'common ground'.

It was in this spirit of unbelief about the perfectibility of relationships that we began our programme of research. What began almost ten years ago as a collaborative enquiry with a group of research partners has since grown into a diverse international community of organizations which, as a result of the insights from the original research, are developing a new language for partnering by working with difference. Instead of trying to find answers to such questions as: 'What makes for a perfect partnership?'; 'How can it be achieved?'; 'What principles should guide the partners in the search for it?', they aim to understand one another. They make no judgments about the merits, or otherwise, of the different perceptions. Instead, they assume that all perceptions are real enough to their perceivers and they use them to discover how understanding and misunderstanding develop.

Although partnering is a subject of great interest to managers in all kinds of organization, it lacks a thought framework to help managers recognize the symptoms and remedy the cause of impending partnership failure. We wanted to provide such a framework, so we assumed at the very outset of our research programme that the basic problems lay not in partnering itself, but in the ways in which partnerships are perceived and therefore managed. We always believed, and nothing we have learned during the research has shaken that belief, that partnering has enormous potential to create value.

We saw in Chapter 1 that the potential returns from partnering are well-worth striving for; but we have seen also that, unless our ambition is matched by our expertise in relationships, failure is pretty well inevitable.

The looser control systems and structures involved in partnering, as opposed to ownership or merger, bring relationship issues into sharp relief. Process integration issues in partnerships have received a lot of attention already; we are interested in the 'human' problems that arise when people work together across organizational as well as functional boundaries.

The partnering grid

The partnering grid plays a central role in this book. It is a new and, in the views of those who have used it, illuminating way of looking at business relationships – and partnerships in particular.

During our research into partnering, we have worked with people from a wide variety of cultural and organizational contexts, ranging from multi-nationals to not-for-profits; from healthcare to banks; from regional government to state-owned companies. The partnering purposes of these organizations are legion, but their perceptions of the challenges are remarkably similar.

Most people see themselves as having been forced into their partnerships by circumstances. They say partnering is more to do with mutual benefit than a wish to co-operate and get on well. Conflict is seen as problematic but inevitable and everyone has a lot to say about it, using words and phrases such as 'adversarial', 'closing ranks', 'territory' and 'empire building'. Partnering language is all too often of 'blame' and 'fault' (never theirs), 'sitting on' information, 'distortion', 'inward looking' and 'managing each other's expectations'.

In short, it is the language of 'power play'.

Throughout our work we have heard most often that problems of power and conflict are not only expected but they are also compounded by the fact that things are never as they appear or as their partners allege. There are always hidden agendas: people feel that their partnerships are too complex to be definable and that it is impossible to get 'everything on the table'.

Five key insights have emerged from our research:

1. Marginalization, not conflict, is what prevents partnerships from suc-
    ceeding. The presence of conflict is not a sign of impending failure and
    neither is its absence a guarantee of success.
2. Things are rarely what they seem. Expectations, perceptions and
    assumptions are the stuff of partnerships and it is the complex interplay
    between them that determines whether a partnership succeeds or
    fails.
3. People associate partnering with 'harmony' and 'synergy'. Values such as
    trust, honesty and integrity are widely seen as vital. But harmony is often
    conspicuous by its absence. Most partnerships generate some and, more
    often, a lot of conflict. Threatening and defensive behaviour is common.
4. Organizations manage conflict in two basic ways – they try to offset it
    by promoting positive values or they try to reduce it by policing
    conformity or achieving homogeneity by seeking partners with very
    similar cultures.
5. Partners usually see difference itself, rather than their response to it, as
    the underlying cause of conflict. But difference can also be a powerful
    source of creativity and transformation. In many cases it is the attempt
    to minimize difference and achieve alignment that creates conflict –
    not difference itself.

These insights led us to develop the 'partnering grid' shown in Figure 2.1.
We will spend most of the rest of this chapter exploring the grid and
explaining the thinking behind it.

Anatomy of the partnering grid

So many deals, diligently researched and expertly structured, end in failure
because the real drivers of partnership dynamics are left largely to chance.
The virtual waters navigated by all corporate relationships are framed by
their ambitions for the partnership, on the one hand, and the way they deal
with difference, on the other.

Ambition, a key component of human energy, is a result of the partners'
views of opportunity and risk. The more the perceptions of risk rise, the
lower the trust expressed. Contrariwise, the greater the opportunity seen
and discussed, the more open and trusting the partners become.

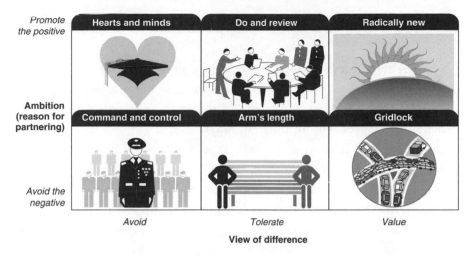

Figure 2.1   *The partnering grid*

Against this we must place the partners' views of difference itself. These can range from avoiding all differences in approach, objectives and values, to actively seeking them out in order to boost innovation and creativity. Most relationships swing unwittingly and unwillingly between these extremes, unable to get a handle on quite how to steer towards mutual benefit.

To explore the intangible elements of their relationship, partners first need a map which enables them to describe and compare the way each sees the partnership and the two key dimensions which drive it.

Partnering grid positions are located by plotting each partner's view of and response to difference, against the reason for entering into the relationship in the first place. Every partnership is predicated on a partnership rationale, or purpose, but the nature of these ambitions varies widely from a wish to prevent negative outcomes (risk management), to the desire to promote positive outcomes (co-creation).

The partners' expectations, perceptions and assumptions around these dimensions are what determine success and failure and it is understanding not smoothing these differences which enables them to manage their relationships more productively.

Let's take a closer look at the hard core of this 'soft' space.

The labels we have given to the boxes should not be seen as the essence of their contents. They are shorthand mottoes to facilitate discussion. What it means to be 'in' a particular box should become clearer as we go along.

Neither should it be assumed that there is an appropriate box for every partner organization. It is neither possible nor desirable to confine a partner to one box, because different people in the same organization will always perceive the partnership in different ways. A box is not a place where a partnership is or is moving towards. It is a place where one individual perceives it to be.

It is tempting to infer from the grid a 'natural' development path, towards the top right of the grid (*radically new*), which the collective perceptions of all partners should aim for. But words such as 'ought' and 'should' have no place in the vocabularies of those who value difference. We believe that *radically new* is an interesting and important box for many enterprises and will devote much of this book to discussing it, but we do not say it is the goal towards which all partnerships should aspire, irrespective of their environments and objectives.

It would be downright dangerous, for instance, if the relationships between air traffic controllers or nuclear power station operators were in any box other than *command and control*. It is also important to take into account the stage an industry or area of activity is at in its life-cycle (emergent, mature, or declining) when articulating the appropriate box for its relationships.

But although one cannot make general judgments about the merit or otherwise of a particular box, it seems clear to us that the 'context' of the modern business world is changing in ways that favour valuing difference (see Figure 2.2).

If asked to locate the modern management debate on the diagram, most people would have little hesitation in saying it straddled the line dividing the 'Tolerate difference' from the 'Value difference' columns. The words in the central column fit the language of modern management best, but the momentum is to the right. The words on the left, for the moment at least, seem old fashioned.

Nevertheless, images of conflict bombard us from all sides. The newspapers and newscasts are full of accounts of fierce and sometimes violent battles between religious or racial groups; between those who want to build new roads and those who want to preserve the countryside; between those who want to export or hunt live animals and those who feel such practices

Minimizing difference	Managing difference	Valuing difference
• Environment is reasonably stable	• Environment is fiercely competitive	• Environment is complex and constantly changing
• Rate of change is stable	• Rate of change is accelerating	• Rate of change is discontinuous
• Resources are plentiful	• Resources are scarce	• Resources are threatened and must be sustained
• External control is slight or non-existent	• External control is very tight	• External control is exercised through commitment
• Few significant stakeholder groups	• Several significant external stakeholder groups (customers, suppliers, neighbours etc.)	• Numerous significant external stakeholder groups

Figure 2.2 *Context and difference*
Source: Tom Boydell, the Learning Company Project

are cruel and inhumane; between those who want to dump oil rigs and nuclear waste at sea, or test nuclear weapons, and those who object to such 'environmental delinquency'; between those who demand more and those who refuse to give it.

In most organizations, and, indeed, in most societies, it has got beyond the stage when a reasonable strategy for managing difference is to try to minimize it. There is simply too much around. We cannot escape or ignore the demands of others to be heard. In open societies and organizations it is impossible to silence the cacophony of voices, views, values and beliefs. We are obliged by the spirit of our time to abandon all fundamentalism and accept the fact that people perceive reality in different ways and that there is no single view about what should be done which all interested parties will agree to.

In other words, the modern environment is shifting towards a position where we all have to work with difference and where those who can make a virtue of this necessity and value difference will have a significant competitive advantage.

This obliges us to look at difference differently – to accept that it is OK to have a different view and that differences, far from being constraints on strategy, are integral parts of the context from which strategy emerges. It is, after all, much easier to change the objectives of a partnership than it is to change the nature of the partners.

So although we can never identify the 'best' box without reference to the partners' specific context, we can say that the prevailing business environment drives organizations to move eastward across the grid. Each perception has its appropriate box, but organizations are increasingly obliged to enter into relationships where power is widely distributed and where it is necessary to value difference. It is not that the boxes on the right are better in some ways than those on the left; it is that organizations are getting involved in relationships where the approaches of the left-hand boxes simply do not work.

In other words, we see *radically new* as a special place where the exigencies of the future are fully confronted. We cannot say any box is the right box, but we can say that, at a time when creativity is both more desirable and more elusive, the most effective relationships are those in which action is based on a search for common ground through dialogue, rather than a search for consensus through persuasion.

The only general prescription offered by the grid is that we should be wary of prescribing. Its value lies in its ability to map the relationship space and allow partners to locate themselves – to understand where they are and to see what options are available.

If partners want change, they should start by changing the way they see difference. The grid gives them a language to do this by discussing the otherwise undiscussable. It is only by sharing our perceptions of ourselves and each other that our own partnering objectives can be scrutinized and realized.

The first imperative for partners is to make the invisible visible – you cannot steer what you cannot define and you cannot define what you cannot talk about.

Let's take a closer a look at the six partnership boxes and the management processes that govern them (see Figure 2.3).

Command and control (bottom left)

From the perspective of *command and control*, the source of most problems encountered in business partnerships and alliances, from the trivial to the life threatening, is difference between the partners. This belief naturally leads to the emergence of strategies aimed at eliminating, or at any rate minimizing, differences in objectives, processes, values and behaviour, typically by

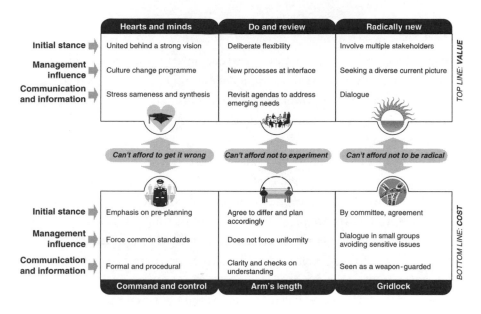

Figure 2.3 *Revealing management processes*

constructing standards and rules and requiring all parties to the relationship to comply with them.

In such partnerships, the relationships are formal and based on negotiated contracts and agreements. There is a belief that every contingency can and must be planned for in advance, in the light of the experiences of previous partnerships. Thus, in *command and control* partnerships, a lot of time must be devoted to pre-contractual preparation to ensure the partnership is 'set up right' in the first place.

It is in the nature of such a relationship that one partner (the one with the most bargaining power) takes charge of drafting these rules. And, because the partnership is just a vehicle for completing a particular transaction, and consists of little more than a formal exchange of resources, skills or whatever form a particular bargain takes, the relationship is generally seen as short term.

The power to get things done is usually centralized and to be found in a small top team where the balance of influence is often weighted in favour of the player who 'owns' the customer; where the management focus is usually on minimizing the risks involved rather than on exploiting the opportunities.

It follows from all this that the characteristics of such partnerships tend to reflect the characteristics of the dominant partner.

Appropriate context

Command and control approaches to partnerships are the obvious choice for relatively hierarchical organizations and a natural end point when there is a significant imbalance of power between partners. That they can work well, and are not inherently fragile, is demonstrated by the success and durability of the Japanese keiretsus where dominant central firms orchestrate the activities of smaller suppliers and sub-contractors.

Adoption of a *command and control* approach can improve the performance of a partnership that begins in another box. The partnering relationship between a healthcare provider and one of its suppliers was fraught with conflict after the organizational re-structuring that brought the partnership into being, but things improved visibly when partners began to focus on their contractual obligations.

The partners came to realize that their initial tacit assumptions about the kind of partnership they were entering were based on a misperception of the new partnering context.

Command and control approaches suit partnerships that lack much ambition or are largely defensive. A hallmark of a defensive partnership is the effort put into planning and preparation. A number of partners involved in a joint venture between two construction companies of much the same size attributed its success to the thoroughness of the formal and legal preparation.

This is a perfectly sensible approach if the prevailing winds bring sudden, singular threat. By highlighting speed and accuracy, the relationship can be focused on a single, fixed target, be that the market or competition. What this approach can never deliver, however, is the sort of innovative agility required in a rapidly changing environment.

Problems and weaknesses

One problem with *command and control* partnerships is that they always assume there is one right view (the dominant partner's) which must be policed, and policing is expensive. A. T. Kearney research suggests that up to 80 % of the time devoted to *command and control* partnership management is accounted for by political activity designed to ensure adherence to the dominant view.

The cost of policing increases with the unpredictability of the environment and thus puts *command and control* partnerships at a serious disadvantage in turbulent environments, such as the advent of new technologies or the opening of new markets.

A second problem is that exercises of *force majeure* in *command and control* partnerships often lead to apportionments of reward that 'junior' partners feel are unfair. Conflicts of interest are endemic in such partnerships and much time and energy must be devoted to managing their effects.

A third problem is that the transactions for which this kind of partnership are the vehicles are often between the top management teams, rather than entire organizations, so typically only a few senior people have a complete picture of what is going on. This exclusivity constrains the argument and mutual exploration that are the main engines of creative co-operation.

The high financial risk associated with a joint construction project in the Far East, for example, encouraged the lead contractor and largest partner to seek a high level of control. This led to conflict and thence litigation reminiscent of the lengthy and very expensive legal squabbles that took place during the construction of the Channel Tunnel.

There are other ways in which the use of a *command and control* approach can poison relationships. The re-structuring of a not-for-profit organization formally separated its two operating divisions. To reflect the new relationship, the managers of one division spent six months drafting a contract with the other and so added emotional distance to the new structural distance. From that point on, the two divisions failed to work effectively together to deliver their joint objectives.

A good example of how the *command and control* approach taken to its extreme can destroy a partnership was the case of a partnership between a part of regional government and a trades union representing employees. Management simply bypassed the unions, thus marginalizing them and pushing the relationship off the grid entirely. It is marginalization, not conflict, which marks the end of a relationship.

Hearts and minds (top left)

In *hearts and minds*, difference is minimized by a search for sameness and alignment, rather than by an imposed structure. The assumption is that if all partners think and feel alike and share a 'culture' they will be able to work together in harmony and produce mutually beneficial outcomes.

'Singing from the same hymn sheet' is a common motto of *hearts and minds* relationships. If everyone is working with the same values towards the same vision, then it is assumed that harmony and creativity will emerge as a result. Hence vision, mission and culture change programmes are often used as the core intervention around which cultures can blend. Striving for sameness leads to a focus on alignment, not only of processes but also of behaviours. Integration through synthesis is the name of the game.

When organizations believe that the articulation of shared visions is the way to win the commitment of their employees, they tend to bring the same philosophy to the partnerships they join. An example of such a philosophy, and the problems it can cause when new contexts present new challenges, is provided by the tale told in Chapter 6 of developments at the Mondragon community of industrial co-operatives in the Basque country, in northern Spain.

Appropriate context

Patient nurturing of a shared culture is regarded, particularly by those whose previous partnering experience has been marked by conflict or confrontation, as the 'correct' approach.

The policy of a virtual network of consultants is to work only with people who share the same values. The success of their business shows such *hearts and minds* relationships can work well.

Some people from the construction companies that worked well together under a carefully planned *command and control* relationship also attributed the joint venture's success to similarities in size and culture, reminding us how different, but compatible, perceptions of the same relationship can co-exist. In this case, the partnership as a whole was clearly in the minimize difference part of the grid, but some people had more ambitious visions for the partnership than others.

An example of how attractive *hearts and minds* can appear to those outside it was provided by partners in a French electronics firm, who attributed their failure to forge a good relationship with a US software company to their very different 'personalities'. Equally, people in the health-care partnership which improved when it switched to *command and control* (see earlier) yearned for *hearts and minds*. They felt it was where they had come from, before the re-structuring, when they and the purchasers were both members of the same organization. It was the contrast between the previous cultural unity and the new cultural divergence which made it so hard for many of them to make sense of, and deal with, the bitter conflicts the new relationship ignited.

Ambitious partnerships between two similar partners tend to find their way to this box and this is the place where relationships between acquirer and acquired companies tend to end up. It is, therefore, a perfectly logical box to choose for a partnership if an acquisition is preferable but impossible (for regulatory or other reasons).

An understandable human trait is to seek out people with whom we feel comfortable, which often means those with whom we share basic beliefs and values. Furthermore, in times of rapid growth, the energy resulting from a compelling shared vision can mobilize people's commitment like no other message. In the right context, one of freedom and plenty, the *hearts and minds* approach can steer a steady course between the need for control and the need for creativity.

Problems and weaknesses

The dangerous weakness in this approach is the extent to which learning is stifled. We learn to check our own assumptions when faced with ones that are different. By forcing such 'dissidence' either underground or to the competition, companies who choose this strategy in the wrong conditions ensure their own downfall.

The problem with this approach to minimizing difference is that while *command and control* openly outlaws difference, *hearts and minds* often simply papers over the cracks and so substitutes a tyranny of culture for a tyranny of power. Conflict goes underground and, because it ceases to exist officially in the homogenized culture, no attempt is made to manage it.

Another problem is that the *hearts and minds* box harbours a logical flaw which can have serious practical consequences. To put it briefly, partners in this box are ambitious for the partnership and ready to invest in establishing and managing it, but most of their investment goes into minimizing the very quality that offers the partnership its best chance of prospering in the long term.

It is very hard to attribute a particular partnership's failure directly to the *hearts and minds* philosophy, because its weaknesses tend to be obscured by the 'cultural homogenization' it seeks and often achieves. Its failures take the form of lost opportunities and tend to show up in general feelings of dissatisfaction and a suspicion that the partnership could have worked better. Such failure is seldom officially recognized, because the mavericks and dissidents who might have given it voice have either been silenced or ejected during the homogenization process.

But if, as suggested earlier, post-acquisition relationships between ac-quirer and acquired are usually of the *hearts and minds* type, indirect evi-dence of the flaws in this approach can be found in the performance of acquisitions. Most researchers, attempting to explain the poor value-creation record of acquisitions in cultural terms, have concluded that the problem is an inadequate homogenization of cultures. In our view, it is more likely that the opposite is the case – that the reason why acquisitions frequently fail to create value is that the acquiring companies refuse to tolerate the differences that are the source of the value they seek.

Arm's length (bottom middle)

Many organizations with *command and control* histories discover, to their initial dismay, that people whose approach is born of other cultures are by and large unchangeable. What seem at first to be clear cases of insubordination become, in time, to be understood as genuine misunderstandings. This leads to a focus on clarity of communication in which meanings and implications are checked and double-checked. Basic identity is cherished and protected. This usually means that any move to get too close is viewed with suspicion – and in this way the partners land firmly in the territory of *arm's length*.

Partners who share this perspective tend to settle any imbalance by agreeing to differ on certain issues so as to give themselves the space they need to pursue other objectives. As understanding of each other's perspec-tive is deliberately limited to the narrow confines of the task in hand, it is common to rely on standard legal and procedural protocols for managing the interface of differences.

There will always be a tendency for collective perceptions of a partner-ship to move to adjacent boxes on the grid as perceivers' views of and responses to difference change.

We have already seen how a partnership that aspires to *hearts and minds* can fail to achieve cultural fusion and, still intolerant of difference, end up in the *command and control* box.

In the same way, *command and control* behaviour can mutate into *arm's length* behaviour when attitudes to difference become more sanguine. Indeed this is, in a sense, an inevitable step when no partner is dominant and when the relationship is expected to continue for some time. It is only possible to suppress the differences between partners for a while. Sooner or later they emerge and, if the partnership is to survive, they must be tolerated.

In the *arm's length* box, this 'relationship risk' is managed by 'agreeing to differ' using careful planning and formal procedures for settling disputes. Good communication, including periodic checks on understanding, is regarded as vital in such partnerships. Flexibility is regarded as valuable, as long as it does not require the loss of too much identity. These relationships tend to be distant and tinged with mild, mutual suspicion.

There is a temporary quality to *arm's length* partnerships. They continue as long as the expected mutual benefits materialize, but partners reserve the moral, as well as the legal, right to withdraw at their convenience or to seek other partners if the relationship gets into difficulties.

Appropriate context

These *arm's length* partnerships are regulated by, and dependent on, external controls and structures, but rely less on policing uniformity. Firms that prefer *command and control* may move to this box reluctantly, after they realize they will have to live with more difference than they would like if they want to work with their partners.

Partners at a European telecommunications company said that they had learned not to rush into a formal contract in case they created loopholes their partner could exploit. They felt that, because they could not control or entirely trust their partner, they had to be free to respond flexibly to every contingency.

Similarly, the special projects division of a civil engineering firm found it impossible to anticipate all contingencies when dealing with off-shore partners. Without regular meetings to check consensus, obscure cultural nuances would cause operational misunderstandings and other problems.

Arm's length works well in changeable environments where the future becomes difficult to predict or where resources become scarce. The approach navigates a course between filling competence gaps, on the one hand, and the need for instant independence, on the other. Dependence is usually inter-preted as unnecessary risk and consequently is avoided with passion. Only those risks that can be equally shared fall into the scope of such a relationship.

Problems and weaknesses

It is this very emphasis on identity which gives this approach strength and amplifies its weakness. Such an emphasis on marking the boundaries of independence leads to blindness to the opportunities which emerge from interdependence. What is never on the agenda cannot be turned into value.

The main weakness of the *arm's length* relationship is that it is defensive and lacks ambition. Partners tolerate each other's idiosyncrasies, but make little effort to establish mutual trust and thus fail to exploit their full potential.

This sense of 'untapped potential' was apparent in the case of two computer manufacturers who were in the habit of piggybacking each other's brands for marketing purposes and had found ways to remain 'civilized' despite the fact that 'we don't trust them an inch'.

The partnership between a European and US airline was similarly con-strained. They delivered into each other's systems, but made no attempt to create an integrated interface, because 'it's important not to concede too much ground'.

It may be argued that the unexploited potential cannot be said to be a flaw in an *arm's length* relationship if the partners had no wish to exploit it. This is reasonable if one assumes the objectives of the partnership are set in stone at the outset. But if there is untapped potential value in such an *arm's length* partnership that could have been released if the partners had been more ambitious and had valued rather than merely tolerated difference, it seems reasonable to suggest there is a flaw in the objective, if not in the relationship itself.

Do and review (top middle)

A relationship that tolerates difference, but takes a longer term view than that of a temporary *arm's length* partnership, needs more committed and more trusting partners. These *do and review* partnerships extend the *arm's length* emphasis on planning and processes from operational to strategic aspects of the relationship.

All partners accept the objectives are conceptual rather than specific and must constantly adapt to new opportunities or threats. There is an ethic of collaboration and co-operation; an assumption the partnership is long term; and a focus on learning and continuous improvement of all the partnership's processes and systems.

The provisional qualities of the *arm's length* relationship are less evident in *do and review* partnerships. There is a sense of sharing a future as well as a present. Such relationships still move step by step and from project to project, but the purpose of the reviews following each step is to learn how to partner better, rather than to decide whether the partnership should continue.

In a *do and review* partnership, deliberate flexibility is encouraged so as to enable both parties to adapt to changing conditions and objectives and, above all, to each other. Learning is seen as a major tool and most actions are reviewed to see what can be learned. Knowledge sharing and the tracking of good practice are seen as essential to survival. Furthermore, the explicit effort to understand each other's positions and priorities strengthens the durability of the relationship and widens the opportunity set for joint projects.

Appropriate context

The *do and review* approach excels at responding to turbulent, highly competitive environments. Partners steer between change on the one hand, and stability on the other, by focusing energy on the virtues of adaptability. This works in relatively well understood conditions where the imperative is direct competition.

Partners in this box describe their relationships as trusting, are ready to go out of their way to cement trust and all have a clear picture of what is going on.

This is a popular box. Our research revealed numerous examples of the *do and review* relationship, where partners make considerable efforts to understand each other's positions.

An electronics firm, for example, had a partnership and alliances director who regularly visited established partners to discuss changing market needs and identify new opportunities.

Before drawing up its strategic plan, a regional government's planning department held a series of workshops to seek the views of partners and then modified their objectives in the light of their findings.

Although generally more comfortable in *command and control* and *arm's length* relationships, a multinational construction group helped a small sub-contractor with a technical problem and so saved him the expense of a consultant engineer. This suggests that, although one company may prefer a particular box, there will always be embryos or potentials of different kinds of relationship.

A long-term partnership between a European computer group and a US software firm runs a permanent, virtual partnership 'conference' on Lotus Notes to facilitate joint learning and to generate rapid feedback about how each of the partners feels joint projects are progressing.

This project orientation of *do and review* relationships was also evident in the 'virtual corporation' of consultants, which holds regular meetings to reflect on the success, or otherwise, of their projects and to learn how to work better together in the future.

Problems and weaknesses

The aims of *do and review* partnerships are often prodigious, but are rarely radical. The step-by-step quality of *do and review* relationships shows the joint quest is for incremental rather than transformational achievement.

This suggests that although *do and review* has a lot going for it, it offers a partial solution at best to the problem of 'untapped potential' in *arm's length* partnerships just discussed. In this case, even more could be achieved if partners valued, rather than merely tolerated, difference.

In other words, although the ambitions of *do and review* relationships are long-term ambitions, they lack depth. The purpose of the efforts to achieve mutual understanding is to make the relationship work more efficiently, not to explore the maximum potential value of the association.

In the current climate of radical transformation, where co-operation is becoming the major competitive agent, it can also become a serious drain on entrepreneurial spirit. While detailed process analysis enables much shared learning, it also tends to inhibit rapid strategic response by stressing the quest for incremental change.

Partners often find themselves with excellently researched, documented and improved processes that bear little or no relation to the emerging demands of a radically new environment. Without a robust mechanism exploiting differences at both strategic and operational levels, *do and review* partnerships must content themselves with learning to do things better, but never to do better things.

Gridlock (bottom right)

There are times in the life of all partnerships where the differences between partners are both respectfully acknowledged and rigorously avoided. It would be naïve to suppose that good intentions inevitably lead to good results, as anyone who has found it necessary to maintain the delicate balance of power in situations of extreme instability will know. Conflicts of interest and half-hidden multiple agendas are to be expected where risk is high and external constraints fierce.

Partners in this context tend to vote for compromise, not by their actions but by the inertia born of their sense of powerlessness and fragmented purpose. Damage limitation, not opportunity, drives this particular dynamic as risks are often experienced as having life or death implications. The inevitable outcome is *gridlock*.

Gridlock is generally an unstable position. When differences are seen as valuable resources, two things can happen. Creative potential is realized and the relationship adopts a more ambitious purpose (moving to *radically new*), or creative potential does not materialize, because of conflict, poor management, or incompatible ideas about the distribution of power and partners will become less convinced of the value of difference and move to the left of the grid (to *arm's length* or *command and control*).

But despite the intrinsic tendency for *gridlock* to drift to other locations, nevertheless we found a lot of inertia in this box. To see the creative potential and recognize the need to respect and work with different views and agendas is not necessarily to know what to do. These partnerships are so constrained by their extreme political instability that they often feel incapable of acting for fear of sinking the boat. Partners are obsessed with the internal dynamics – they often fall into the trap of trying to fix and change each other rather than focusing their energy on fixing the task.

Gridlock occurs when power is widely distributed. It fosters compromise and efforts to keep the peace and ensure no one 'loses face'. Its effect is to add to the fragmentation of power a fragmentation of *purpose* and to focus attention on power and face saving rather than the task at hand. People in *gridlock* are so pre-occupied with the relationship itself, they can forget what it is for.

Appropriate context

The appropriateness or otherwise of this box will depend on the stability in the partnership. If, for instance, instability is such that any move, by any partner, might blow the whole thing apart, this box might be preferable to boxes to the left of it, particularly if the number of partners is large and the configuration is complex.

A *gridlock* perception is very unlikely to be shared by every constituent in the partnership, however, and the extent to which partners are content with this box often has more to do with a reluctance to lose their autonomy than with an objective assessment of the system's fragility.

The way partners perceive their contexts are very deeply ingrained in their general outlooks, including the differences they see, and whether partners see themselves in *gridlock*, or the more creative *radically new* box, depends on the lens they are looking through when making the judgment.

When face saving becomes more important than joint action, and high political activity makes an unwelcome appearance, it is usually read by all parties as heralding impending failure.

This is an enormously oversimplified view and a catastrophic mistake.

Steering between stability and instability is a precarious business. People who are severely constrained by circumstances truly beyond their control have no option but to try to freeze the joint potential for long enough to allow the situation to stabilize. This is a natural, sensible and even respectful response to the sort of volatile conditions that would otherwise blow the venture sky high.

Furthermore, for the positive potential of a gridlocked situation to be seen and acted on, uncompromising straight talk about purposes is required. Without a concerted effort to reveal the motives behind the actions, there are no stars by which to steer. Success here requires courage and integrity; and courage and integrity in the face of adversity are to be applauded, not disbanded.

Problems and weaknesses

The problems and weaknesses of *gridlock* are largely superficial. The more a partner looks at difficulties, the more they appear to him or her to be part of the relationship itself. Those who see themselves in this box are likely to be adopting defensive attitudes against their will or better judgment.

It is unlikely, therefore, that all the partners would be content to remain in *gridlock* and so deny themselves, and each other, a chance to capture the value they see in their differences, particularly as the alternative is the gradual dissolution of the partnership.

If *gridlock* is a response to temporary but extreme volatility, then it is not to be feared and interpreted as problematic. The danger arises when the high level of risk disables partners from telling it as it is. The outward appearance of *gridlock* is often the result of real or perceived hidden agendas aimed at subtle domination of one partner over another. In such circumstances, relationships deteriorate to such an extent that the only workable options are retreat, rebellion or apathy.

Acknowledging and respecting differences in such conditions then becomes a game people play to strengthen their own position in the perpetual argument about who is right. A partnership in name only, the obsession with posturing prevents partners from identifying, let alone working on, the one thing that can break the deadlock – a mutually compelling task on which all can work without first having to change themselves.

Radically new (top right)

Some partners actively seek out differences of all kinds: operational, industrial, professional and cultural *and* make it work. Often highly innovative and creative partnerships, this *radically new* approach puts a premium on challenge, dialogue and democracy.

By involving and acting on the views of multiple stakeholders, *radically new* partners, or more often networks of partners, are able to respond instantaneously to the changing demands of an unpredictable world. Those who have developed the intellectual and cultural agility to thrive in such circumstances are usually compelled by their business contexts to reinvent themselves afresh.

When differences are not only valued, but are also welcomed, partners begin to see their relationship as, if not yet a solution, at least a place where a solution might be found to the most pressing problem of all: the need for organizations to change themselves to cope with a turbulent present and an unpredictable future.

In these circumstances, the partnership becomes not just an adjunct to each partner's ways of being, but an integral part of their identity. Difference is valued and the perspectives of everyone in the partnering organizations contribute to and help define the relationship. Instead of seeking shared visions of the future, partners seek pictures of the shared present through an understanding of each other's views and values.

Partners cease to try to change or convert each other (that would take them back to *hearts and minds*) and embark instead on a joint search for 'common ground' on which, despite their differences (or because of them), there are possibilities for joint action.

The partnership is not defined; it is allowed to emerge from the day-to-day experience of working together. All the feelings of separateness that made *gridlock* so uncomfortable and frustrating are abandoned and a shared sense of destiny comes to dominate the outlook of all those involved.

Radically new is, in a way, the ultimate box: the place where difference is valued so much and partners' sights are set so high that the full creative potential of the relationship becomes accessible.

Such thoroughgoing partnerships remain rare, but our research provided some examples of partnerships that exhibited some of the qualities of *radically new*, if not yet the full-blown reality.

The overseas division of a not-for-profit organization convened a three-day local partners' forum in Kenya and invited local groups competing for its resources to set the agenda and suggest changes to the organizer's way of doing business.

As part of its campaign to promote environmental regeneration, a regional government's planning department created a 'space' in which everyone's views and concerns were openly discussed. The space obliged politicians, officers and local community groups to find new ways of working together.

Appropriate context

A *radically new* relationship is necessary when both power and knowledge are so widely distributed between the partners that no other kind of relationship will work. E-ventures and alliances often demand such a radical perspective if real value is to emerge from the virtual plans.

It may also be appropriate in other contexts, when those with the power recognize that the full creative potential of the partnership they seek to exploit will not be realized until they learn that their power alone cannot make things happen.

The interconnected nature of the issues faced by both governments and business in times of discontinuity means that unless the complex interplay of accountabilities, rights and obligations is addressed in *radically new* ways, partnering efforts will fragment into *gridlock*, not into action.

Steering a tentative course between a shared sense of direction, on the one hand, and volatile unpredictability, on the other, requires a very pragmatic mindset and the commitment of all involved. Strategy as such emerges and is rooted in what people can do together in spite of, or perhaps even because of, their differences.

Problems and weaknesses

An excessive respect for difference for its own sake can sometimes lead to inaction, because nothing is clear, nothing can be resolved and dialogue ends in bland compromises and agreements to differ.

And *radically new* can be risky also because it obliges partners to exchange their old identities for a new, collective identity. They have to put their fates in each other's hands and, if the partnership fails, it is almost impossible for each partner to emerge unscathed.

Moreover, because it is an emergent rather than a deliberate fusion of ways of being, *radically new* can creep up on you. You may not be aware that the growing intimacy of the partnership has eroded your organization's sense of self until it is much too late to halt the process. The tendency to move up the partnering grid as trust develops, and to become more collectively ambitious, weakens the cultural 'glue' that binds employees to their organizations. Loyalty and commitment can seep away from the partners and become vested in the partnership.

The strength of *radically new* is, of course, its weakness. It works well in conditions where power, know-how and purpose are widely distributed *and* there is a strong sense of connected purpose. It is, however, highly unstable and steadfastly refuses to respond to plan. The optimum approach for seeing and growing new knowledge, it is perhaps the least suited to exploiting it.

In the search for the ultimate organizational design, such pockets of creativity are often recommended as the blueprint for the knowledge-based, e-driven economy and herein lies the danger.

Solidarity is not an enforceable quality. Pinning down behaviours and working out how to make them happen ensures compliance, but does not guarantee commitment. And this, of course, kills the very creativity it is intended to harness. *Radically new* works if and when the conditions demand it, but it can never deliver control.

Every partnership is complex because it always consists of many individual perceptions that differ widely between and within member organizations. The way the financial controller of one partner organization, for example, sees the partnership may be much closer to the way his or her opposite number in the partner organization sees it, than to the way that his or her own human resources colleagues perceive it.

The grid's diagnostic power lies in its ability to reduce these perceptions to what we believe are the two most important dimensions of partnering; the two dimensions that when combined illuminate the unspoken assumptions about what partnership in general, and this particular partnership, mean.

Sometimes the diagnosis will reveal that all is well and the partnership is perceived in ways that are appropriate for its context and objectives. But the decision to do the diagnosis suggests that, in most cases, it will give substance to fears that something is wrong and indicate a need for movement in the grid.

We will see how individuals and organizations can move round the partnering grid in search of fit in the next chapter. Before that we invite readers to roadtest it by plotting their perceptions, and those of their colleagues or partners, with the help of a condensed, pen-and-paper version of our partnering diagnostic software (Appendix B).

Story from the front...

A tale of two partnerships

A former executive of a large European transportation company shared with us his reflections on two major alliances he was intimately involved with, using the grid as the framework for his comments.

'The grid is a really useful way of thinking about our relationships, especially the idea that views of difference differ. The only attitude we had was avoidance, or tolerance of difference – most of our strategy was bottom left [*command and control*].

'There was some co-operation, collaboration and sharing of views, but mostly for the purpose of preventing negatives.

'I was involved in the early stages with two major alliances. In both cases, we would have avoided a partnership if it had been possible; we were succumbing to the inevitable. We would have preferred to grow ourselves, in all markets. If we could not do that we would have preferred to buy companies outright, so partnering was really the third best option.

'The first partner didn't like the idea at all; it was forced into it by government. And the other would not have agreed to do it if they had not needed our cash. Our original plan was to buy it outright, but we had to settle for a minority stake. Our culture was very centrist; we preferred to run everything from our head office.

'That changed later; we learned how to do it. The franchising programme (where we have effectively loaned our brand to some smaller companies) would not have been considered in the old days, but it has become more acceptable now. The franchises worked very well, better than the alliances, because we could forget about them. With alliances the wheels are spinning all the time.

'Individuals are moving up the grid and to the right, because continuous exposure forces them to recognize that "these guys are better than us at some things". We realized, for example, that our US partner was much better at operational planning, whereas we were better at the "big picture". They could operate larger networks, with far more customers, and some of our operations people had a lot of exposure to that.

'Because the US style is focused on quarterly results, people are set short-term targets. The European style is less short-term focused and that is a weakness and a strength. It means we're not so good at planning, but also that we're more flexible, and we see the big picture more clearly. While they stuck rigidly to plan, we were willing to throw the plan away for the right reasons.

'Many of our procedures were learned from our US partner; they are much better at operating large sites. There were a lot of other operational things we could have learned from them, had the partnership lasted.

'The company as a whole is staying in the bottom left of the grid, but some individuals see things differently. There are long lags and huge dampers on getting that to the company, however. It may learn from individuals eventually but it will take a long time.

'The idea that you can have partnership and no control – that you can get a high degree of partnership, with a low level of legal involvement – was part of the original vision, but it needed both companies to move significantly to the middle and top right of the grid.

'Some early discussions seemed quite promising. We got senior officers from both companies locked away, and discussed what might be possible. It got to a position where the long-term perspective was that we should operate as a single company to all intents and purposes. But if people are not seeing each other every week such visions fade, and anything that goes wrong is immediately seen as a conspiracy rather than a cock-up. Trust diminishes exponentially if you don't see people.

'We needed a greater feeling of common purpose within the two companies. For most people, the primary allegiance was to the company; the partnership was secondary. My team felt the other way round, but we were the exceptions.

'The partnership degenerated to a minimum "maintenance" level with just enough contact to keep the business relationship going. It was a great pity. I gave two years of my life to it and I still think the potential benefits were huge.

'The distancing began way before we sold the shares. It began with a difference of opinion between the CEOs on further cash injections. Their position was: "Trust us to sort it out, but we need more cash." We switched from being a white to a black knight, when our CEO refused to subscribe to a rights issue. That seemed like a betrayal to them – they felt right through the company that they had been deceived, let down.

'The other partner didn't want us but their government wanted a trade investor, and we were seen as the least bad option. Things changed when a new CEO took over and brought in a new management team. They wanted a joint service agreement, and we acquired a common enemy in the government, and became closer. But it was hard to be really close when there was so little common office time.

'The relationship has had its ups and downs but it was always a much more "instrumental" partnership than the one with the US company. Both sides were getting something out of it. They didn't feel we were the dominant partner so the conversations were between grown-ups. But it was much shallower than the US relationship; there is little co-operation beyond the service agreement and we were all too busy to think seriously about how it might be deepened.

'An important issue, when choosing your partners, is how much you can trust them. We spoke to most of the major companies in our sector. Some had partners already, but said they would drop them for us – that makes you wonder how trustworthy they are. The trust you get is the trust you earn.

'You also have to deal with intra-company differences between departmental cultures. That is a big issue if a company wants to move to the top right of the partnering grid. We had often been very departmentalized, when different departments insist on sticking to procedures laid down for the relationship, but at other periods there has been a lot of rule breaking, risk taking and opening up.

'It would be very useful to develop a mechanism for moving in the grid; finding new ways to initiate movement. In my view, the way to move is to have lots of face-to-face meetings, so people have more opportunities to feel "they're just like us" or "they're different, but the difference is valuable". It is like unilateral disarmament. Don't wait until your company says it is OK to share information – do it now. It is very difficult, however, because people have to take personal risks, and then convince their company after the event.

'We were good in short periods of crisis when everyone had to focus on immediate action and people had to trust each other. The work was managed differently. There was much more emphasis on customer service, and management was very open with staff and other areas; the whole company was more open. There was a lot of risk taking and rule breaking.'

3

Searching for fit

*I should be happy, myself, to propose two
months . . . but I have a partner, Mr Jorkins*
Charles Dickens, *David Copperfield*

The partnering grid described in Chapter 2 identifies six basic partnership
cultures defined by 'ambition' on the vertical axis and 'attitude to difference' on the horizontal, which can be used to analyse individual and
collective perceptions of any partnership.

Perceptions are not facts, but a set of perceptions can reveal the
differences between partners and, by illuminating a relationship, help
partners understand each other better and work together more effectively.

In this chapter we will see how leaders can use the grid to assess how far
their and their partners' perceptions of the partnering relationship suit the
'context' of the partnership; we will explore steps to improve fit and see how
the power and knowledge characteristics of the partners help determine the
most appropriate moves.

Context is determined by three factors – the external environment in
which the partnering occurs, the personalities of the partnering organizations
(their cultures and distributions of power and knowledge) and the objective
of the partnership (see Figure 3.1). For example, *command and control* is a
perfectly appropriate box for a relationship where power and knowledge are
concentrated, but far less appropriate (and therefore less effective) if power
and knowledge are widely distributed. Similarly, *command and control* suits a
defensive relationship, designed to preserve the status quo, but not an ambitious relationship that seeks synergy and co-creation.

	Environment	Style	Objectives
Command and control	• Immediate threat • Predictable knowledge environment • Little external regulation • Few significant stakeholders • Widely available resources	• Preference for formality, structure, compliance • Power comes from the top • Knowledge distribution based on bureaucracy and hierarchy	• Response to low choice situation (e.g. bankruptcy, takeover) • Maintain stability and manage risk (e.g. integration of operations)
Hearts and minds	• Steady incremental growth opportunities • Predictable, knowable environment • Little external regulation • Few significant stakeholders • Widely available resources	• Preference for harmony, shared vision • Unitary, dominant power • Limited knowledge distribution, held in cultures and values	• Optimize existing products/ services in existing markets • New products/services in existing markets • Explore new markets with aligned cultures

Arm's length	• External barriers to operations (e.g. regulatory, cultural)
	• Growing unpredictability
	• Tight regulation
	• Widening stakeholder community
	• Strong competition
	• Scarce resources
		• Preference for minimal movement
		• Focus on clear communication
		• Sharing of power, control and ownership in order to share risks
		• Knowledge widely distributed, centrally held and orchestrated
			• Minimal partnerings to:
			  – Overcome external barriers
			  – Reduce costs
			  – Share risks

Do and review	• Turbulent change, significant expansion opportunities
	• Growing unpredictability
	• Tight regulation
	• Widening stakeholder community
	• Strong competition
	• Scarce resources
		• Preference for collaboration, learning, flexibility
		• Strong process orientation
		• Sharing of power, control and ownership
		• Knowledge widely distributed, attempts at central sense making
			• Technological/product innovation in new markets
			  – Incremental change
			  – Cyclical improvements
			• Expansion within turbulent markets

Gridlock	• Strong constraining external forces (regulatory, market) • Multiple influential stakeholders • Resources threatened	• Preference for control by commitment • Knowledge treated as private: seen to be fragmented and held within power bases	• Compromise to stabilize political situation • Defence against conflicting purposes • Keeping everyone happy: face saving paramount
Radically new	• Complex, discontinuous change • Low predictability • Broad and influential stakeholder community	• Preference for involvement, challenge and dialogue • Power and ownership accepted as widely spread • Knowledge is treated as public: seen to reside within network of relationships	• Pre-empt change with degree and speed of innovation • Create radically new ways of working and/or product/service offerings • Optimize creativity and transformation

Figure 3.1 *Partnering contexts*

Misjudging the appropriate culture is a common cause of partnering failure and the most common misjudgment of context is to assume, and to act as if, you have more power than you actually have. When a partnership goes wrong it is usually because someone in control has misjudged the context and adopted an approach or style that is at odds with how others perceive the distribution of power and knowledge.

To establish the 'fit' of your partnering culture to its context, start by asking your partners which box they think you are in. To determine fit in a partnership, you have to talk and discuss. You are not where you think are; you are where others perceive you to be.

Improving fit

One of the most striking results of our research was how eager people were to find 'the answer' to partnering. Most wanted a standard, general purpose solution, despite the fact that the research clearly showed some approaches to partnering were widely seen to be more successful in some contexts than in others.

It is important to resist the natural temptation to view movement up and to the right of the grid as a developmental process. The appropriateness of a box depends on the context, what drove each partner to join the partner-ship in the first place and on what inspires them to remain in it.

Environment is part of the context and the appropriateness of a particular grid location depends partly on environmental qualities such as stability, resource availability, external controls (e.g. regulation), pattern of owner-ship, the influence of non-owning constituencies and, above all, on the distribution of power.

The dimension on the grid that must 'fit' context is view of difference. It is 'horses for courses'. In some contexts, minimizing difference is fitting while in others tolerating or valuing difference is more appropriate.

Hearts and minds and *command and control* are suitable if the environment is stable and predictable. Those with power know what needs to be done and see their task as ensuring that it is done well.

If the world becomes less predictable, and people begin to realize that, if the enterprise cannot learn as fast as its environment is changing it may perish, *do and review* or *arm's length* will become more suitable and efforts will have to be made to construct feedback loops, get everyone 'closer to the customer' and use so-called 'boundary workers' to scan the environment and gather intelligence.

Building on the model developed by Tom Boydell of the Learning Company Project (see Figure 2.2) allows us make general observations about the sorts of style most appropriate to different contexts.

Difference-minimizing organizations seek stability and often attempt to use partnerships to 'stabilize' environments they find uncomfortably volatile. The partnering styles in *hearts and minds* and *command and control* are both transactional, but the objectives differ. The *hearts and minds* organization enters partnerships to achieve goals it could not have achieved on its own, while the *command and control* organization tends to see its partnering as a way of managing risk.

Difference-managing organizations always seek adaptability in turbulent and competitive environments. Partnering styles in both *do and review* and *arm's length* are process oriented, but their objectives differ. The *do and review* organization enters into partnerships to adapt to a new or changed context and pursue goals it could not have pursued on its own, whereas *arm's length* organizations see partnering as a way to 'manage' risk by sharing it.

Difference-valuing organizations also seek to keep themselves fully adapted to turbulent or unpredictable environments, but do so through collaborative advantage (different from competitive advantage, in that they work with their environment rather than try to dominate it). Partnering styles in *radically new* and *gridlock* both focus attention on the relationship itself, but the beliefs differ. *Radically new* partners believe that wonderful things could and probably will happen. *Gridlock* partners believe wonderful things could but probably won't happen. Partners in *gridlock* often help to fulfil their own pessimistic prophesies by refusing to abandon their own agendas in the interests of preserving 'stability'.

Movement in the grid becomes necessary if it is clear that the existing box or style is unsuited to the environment (either because the environment was not understood at the outset or because it has changed) or if the style is unsuited to the objectives, either because this element of fit was not recognized at the outset or because objectives have changed (because they have been achieved or because the partners wish to embark on projects that require a closer, longer term relationship).

Appendix C provides a simple tool to help you and your partners surface and discuss the context in which you are operating and to debate the fit of your various partnering styles to that context.

But it is far easier to describe the circumstances in which movement in the grid is desirable than to recognize and respond to them. For one thing, it is often hard to know when the environment changes and different object-ives become more suitable and, for another, most companies lack the chameleon's ability to adapt instantly to a new environment. They become wedded to and comfortable with a particular partnering style and even when the weaknesses of *command and control* become obvious, for example in a partnership where both power and knowledge are widely distributed, it can be hard to come to terms with the need to replace an organization's central 'brain' with a new kind of system that can distil collective interpret-ations from many views.

One thing is clear: if a lack of fit between style and objectives is not addressed, you may be sure that, over time, it is not culture that will change the better to meet its objectives – objectives will be distorted and diluted to adapt to the prevailing culture. For example, a *command and control* manufacturer partnered with a *do and review* service provider to deliver new IT services that were seen as a new lease of life for the manufacturing organization. However, it was not long before tension and mistrust were the order of the day. At one point in the contract, the service provider had 80 members of staff delivering to the manufacturer – and the manufacturer had 100 of its own staff checking on their delivery. New services were no more than a distant memory. The prevailing *command and control* culture remained entrenched and the ambitious goals slipped back to accommodate it.

The tension between a partner's perception of the context and its preferred style is an important dynamic in partnering. It does not mean styles always have to be sacrificed on the altars of context, but it does mean position on the grid should never be taken for granted.

Take the case of an organization that decides the only way to compete is to form a partnership to develop new, leading edge products. Its environment is risky and highly regulated and thus more suited to a project-based *do and review* style, but its partner prides itself on having a *radically new* style well suited to innovation.

The organization has a number of options. It can:

- test the validity of its view of the partnering environment by asking other interested parties for their perceptions
- review the partnership's objectives in the light of new information and modify them, if necessary
- try to adapt its partnering style more fully to the context.

If the testing validates the organization's original view, and if the value of the potential additional revenues and the potential fortification of its market position are considered too valuable to relinquish, the organization has no option but to take its fate in its hands and try to navigate the grid.

Navigating the grid

First a word of warning for grid navigators: our research suggests that the bottom left and bottom right boxes are both powerful attractors in which it is easy to get stuck.

Static, under-managed partnerships tend to drift to the left, because of a tendency to leave partnership management to conventional gatekeepers, such as accountants and lawyers whose professions predispose them to *command and control* styles.

We also found a strong pull to the bottom right. As the wider distributions of power, knowledge and purpose transform the business environment more and more, partnerships find no one party has control over enough of the agenda to navigate a straight course. As each partner defends its patch and tries to control the outcomes, the partnership slips deeper into *gridlock*.

This is both bad and good news: bad, because to remain in *gridlock* for long can often be fatal for the partnership (*command and control* at least has the merit of being able to insist on action); and good because, apart from the crucial inability to let go of the illusion of control, all the other elements of a creative, *radically new* partnership are in place.

If an organization needs to improve its 'fit', and wants to avoid being captured by the *command and control* and *gridlock* attractors, it needs to understand the dynamics influencing its own position and those of its partners.

Once a partnership perception has been located on the grid (for a first-cut position try the simple test described in Appendix B), there are three directions in which it can move: vertically along the ambition axis, horizontally along the view of difference axis and diagonally along both axes simultaneously (see Figure 3.2).

It is important to recognize, however, that starting positions (of partners and the partnership itself) are never universal. The grid plots perceptions and there are all sorts of different ways in which partnerships are seen by the partners themselves and by outsiders. When we say a partner or a partnership is in a certain box, we are saying that, from the point of view of this person or group, this is where the partner or partnership *seems* to be.

But the subjective nature of a grid position does not prevent movement. All it says is that the direction and extent of movement is also subjective and will be perceived differently by different people. Movement on the grid is a mental, not a physical event. It occurs as a result of conversations and becomes apparent in changes in behaviour and the ways people talk about the relationship and act within it.

It is also important to recognize that movements in the grid are rarely the results of deliberate intent. Movement occurs when the veil of ignorance

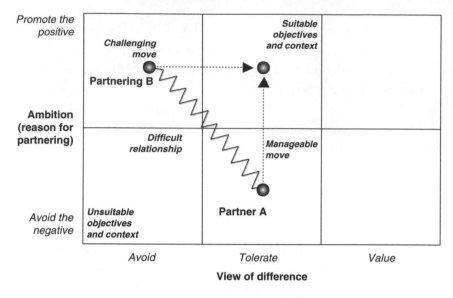

Figure 3.2 *Partnering moves*

about the motivations and beliefs of everyone involved in the partnership is lifted or lowered. Ignoring your assumptions and those of your partner, or keeping them private, will result in movement down and to the left. Becoming more aware of those assumptions, and making them public, will result in movement up and to the right.

Moving diagonally

Moving diagonally is difficult because two partners in diagonally adjacent boxes perceive different realities and will find it hard to form productive relationships without major adjustments to their general outlooks.

But this does not mean that diagonal partnering must or can be avoided. Whether or not a change in perceptions is appropriate depends less on how hard it is to change and more on how far existing perceptions are from perceptions that fit the context.

A diagonal movement is the most challenging since it is a combination of a vertical and a horizontal move: two significant shifts in understanding and attitude. The challenge is to cut loose from existing perceptions, resist the siren calls of the attractors at the bottom left and bottom right of the grid and head in a north-easterly direction. Once in motion, partner perceptions need to be actively steered not merely towards the desired positions, but also away from the default positions.

To build a clearer picture of the composite diagonal shift, we need to look at the dynamic natures of vertical and horizontal 'movement' more closely.

Moving vertically

Vertical is easier than horizontal movement, because partners occupying boxes directly above or below each other are usually more compatible and can form stable relationships more readily.

But, because the quality that drives vertical movement up the grid is trust and trust is easy to lose, it is movement that can quickly be reversed.

For example, partners who dislike difference, but are ambitious for the partnership, may decide *command and control* is too constraining and attempt to move to *hearts and minds*. If trust fails to develop, or either partner feels that their trust is betrayed or not fully reciprocated, the relationship is likely either to come to an end or to revert to *command and control*.

A study by Bleeke and Ernst found that about 80% of joint ventures end in a sale by one partner to the other.[1] In the language of the grid, this suggests a strong tendency for power to become more concentrated as a partnership develops and for the style of those with the power to default to *command and control*. This is natural; *command and control* is appropriate when power becomes concentrated in the hands of one partner, as it tends to do when a partnership runs into difficulties.

As already noted, there is a time element in vertical movement, in the sense that an ambitious partnership tends to be perceived as long term. It is this anticipated longevity that makes it worth spending the time it may take to cultivate trust which, in principle at any rate, is a more efficient way to ensure reciprocity than a tightly worded, vigilantly policed contract.

On being asked which leg it moved first, the centipede became rooted to the spot. Trust is like that – the more one focuses on it, the more elusive it becomes. Trust and the lack of it are not the causes of success and failure in partnering; they are symptoms. They emerge from the way people speak and act with each other and the only way to foster the emergence of trust is to find new ways of talking and acting.

Those who have used the grid have said it provides a way to talk about the foundations of trust without talking about trust itself. Some have found it better to compare and discuss differences in grid positions than to try to build trust without this practical and objectified context.

A focus on trust itself often creates a culture of blame and suspicion that makes things worse. Trust comes from action. We need to turn the focus from the relationship to the task and find tasks we can agree on. Trust emerges spontaneously from working together successfully.

The way to build trust is to become more trustworthy, by being honest about your motives. The 'conscience' of each partner can be strengthened through, for example, joint teams charged with recording the partnership's learning history. Outsiders can be helpful here, because they will be less inclined to re-write history to suit specific political purposes. For the same reason, some have found that appointing a neutral third party to act as ombudsman and arbitrator has had a powerful effect on partnering success.

Disconnections in the vertical dimension often reflect differences in how risk is perceived. Reaching an understanding of how risks and opportunities are seen by each partner, and establishing mechanisms for updating it, can help to add upward momentum to perceptions. Standard risk assessment tools, that allow parties to state their opinions of quantitative and qualitative risk, can also enhance mutual understanding, but some credence should also be given to intuition because 'gut feel' often has more impact on behaviour and perceptions than data.

One reason for the power of the bottom left attractor is that it is all too easy for partners to become locked in discussion habits that make vertical movement difficult to initiate and maintain. If every proposal is greeted with a chorus of 'Yes, but...,' the most optimistic of partners will find it hard to maintain their initial enthusiasm. Employing techniques such as De Bono's six 'thinking hats,'[2] which insist on the recognition of opportunity before the statement of risk, can help sustain upward momentum.

Moving horizontally

Although horizontal movement is in many ways more challenging than vertical movement, there is more to be gained from it for two reasons. First, because moving from minimizing to tolerating difference widens partner choice and, second, because tolerating differences makes relationships more robust. We have found that, in partnerships where power and knowledge are both widely distributed, moving partnership perceptions horizontally across the view of difference dimension in pursuit of a better 'fit' with context is much the most effective way to improve partnership performance.

If you want to change, in other words, change the way you see difference.

The difficulty with 'horizontal' movement is that people tend to cling more fiercely to their views of difference than to their partnership ambitions. Everyone is for trust, just as everyone is against sin, but the benefits of linking up with an alien culture and running the risk of cultural infection are less compelling. By and large, *command and control* and *hearts and minds* cultures will be reluctant to move to *arm's length* and *do and review*, while other options remain available.

The reason for this reluctance to move to the right of the grid is that it demands much more of people. They must abandon basic assumptions about how their firms operate and change what Argyris and Schon call their 'theories in use' as opposed to their 'espoused theories' of difference.[3] People who say they tolerate, or even value difference (espoused theory), but then try to minimize it (theory in use) must focus more on action and less on lip service before they can move to the right of the grid.

The globalization of business is putting pressure on organizations to 'bite the bullet' of easterly movement, because a refusal to move to the right is a self-imposed strategic straitjacket. No organization that refuses to form partnerships with organizations that have developed within foreign cultures can aspire to be truly 'global'.

Figure 3.3 shows how the shifts from minimizing to managing, and from managing to exploiting difference challenge various assumptions about how enterprises are organized, and highlights the implications of an intent to move in the horizontal plane. When people acknowledge that power is widely distributed, but continue to treat systems as given, insist on removing uncertainty and differences, impose their organization's persona or sense of self from the top or learn only from their own experiences, they are being unrealistic or disingenuous and have a long way to go before they can achieve horizontal movement.

We must emphasize again that movement from left to right of the grid is not a 'natural' development path. Movement can be in any open direction and the merits or otherwise of a particular box depend on context. The only test of the suitability of a box is whether or not it works. If *command and*

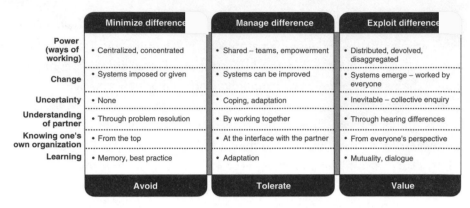

	Minimize difference	Manage difference	Exploit difference
Power (ways of working)	• Centralized, concentrated	• Shared – teams, empowerment	• Distributed, devolved, disaggregated
Change	• Systems imposed or given	• Systems can be improved	• Systems emerge – worked by everyone
Uncertainty	• None	• Coping, adaptation	• Inevitable – collective enquiry
Understanding of partner	• Through problem resolution	• By working together	• Through hearing differences
Knowing one's own organization	• From the top	• At the interface with the partner	• From everyone's perspective
Learning	• Memory, best practice	• Adaptation	• Mutuality, dialogue
	Avoid	**Tolerate**	**Value**

Figure 3.3   *Revealing assumptions*

control works, don't try to fix it. Moving in the grid requires profound changes in attitudes to power, knowledge and learning and, as weather forecasters say after a snow warning: 'Don't travel unless it is absolutely necessary.'

In summary then, movement in the grid can take the form of an unintentional slip or a deliberate step to improve fit. Movement can often be started by plotting the current positions of the partners on the grid, because just talking about difference in grid language can inspire some horizontal movement.

Many people who have used the grid say that it is particularly helpful with relationship issues, but that although it is quite easy to locate your own styles on the grid, it is harder to locate the styles of partners, because without dialogue (of which more later) it is easy to mistake a *command and control* player, say, for a *hearts and minds* or *do and review* player.

Understanding your partners is hard and is made even harder because it is sometimes in their interests to masquerade as someone else. Even when no deception is intended, the style displayed in the early stages of a relationship may not represent the partner's true self, in the same way that firms that put all their efforts into selling make promises about after sales service they are not equipped to keep.

The following rough-and-ready guide to partnering styles should help you to 'read' your partners better.

Understanding each other

In *hearts and minds* and *command and control*, the conceptions partners have of themselves are provided by leaders who have little interest in how their organizations are perceived by their partners. When partners have to do as they are told, there is no need to understand them. Difference is ignored because, as far as the partnership is concerned, there is none. If it nonetheless emerges, it is seen as recalcitrance – at best not playing the game; at worst, deceitfulness. 'Understanding' between partners will only be achieved, according to this view, when difference has been eradicated.

In *arm's length* and *do and review*, people accept that partners differ and realize that the only way for them to understand each other and to learn to work well together despite their differences is to involve everyone in the processes of partnership. So they form inter-company and inter-disciplinary teams, for example, to undertake joint process re-engineering projects or joint customer service reviews and improvement programmes.

Elaborate systems often emerge in the central area of the grid designed to manage interfaces between the processes of each partner and to monitor the quality of understanding so that, although the partners speak in different languages, they can achieve meetings of minds.

On the right of the grid, people are very interested in how their partners see them. They try hard to avoid stereotypes (including those generated by the grid) and achieve an understanding of themselves and of each other.

Bearing these reflections in mind, let's see what clues about where on the grid people are coming from we can glean from our partners' attitudes and behaviour.

Seeing others from hearts and minds

Partners in *hearts and minds* have reason to believe other partners are in:

Command and control, if they tend to insist on doing everything by the book and on everything being in the book; if they do not seem to trust you much and 'build the divorce into the marriage ceremony'; if they exercise their power through written contracts and threats of divorce, and if you feel oppressed by their rules and frustrated by their defensiveness and their slow-moving processes.

Arm's length, if they seem wary of your visions; say 'yes' to your way, but carry on doing things their way; seem distant and secretive about their own values and purposes, and exercise power by refusing to return your calls and insisting on doing things differently, to prove a point.

Do and review, if the agenda changes at each meeting and their need to meet and design processes seems insatiable; if they always appear to be starting their next change project; if they cannot even agree among themselves about what should happen next; if they are always asking for more data; if they keep moving the goalposts; and if they exercise their power by threatening to leave the partnership when you refuse to tell them something.

Gridlock, if they seem unmotivated and lacking in leadership or vision, but refuse to accept your vision; if they veto things just when you are getting enthusiastic; and if they do not try to exercise any power at all and keep retreating into their shell.

Radically new, if they lack conventional leadership and seem indecisive and woolly; if it is hard to see what they want; if they make no sense half the time, but push your 'comfort zones' in unexpected ways; if they seem deeply interested (sometimes alarmingly so) in the ways you do things, and if they exercise power, if you can call it that, by carrying on regardless.

Seeing others from command and control

Partners in *command and control* have reason to believe the other partner is in:

Hearts and minds, if they are always reluctant to put things in writing; if everything seems to be about 'values'; if they all say much the same thing; if they are always talking about 'creativity' and 'synergy'; if they seem blind to threats, and if they exercise their power by quietly excluding you or urging you to accept their vision.

Arm's length, if they make simple things problematic and are always asking you to clarify your position; if they insist on doing things their way, and if they make it clear that they are willing to give so much, and no more.

Do and review, if their demands for information seem presumptuous (they are very nosy); if their rules change each time you meet; if their appetite for change is insatiable; if they seem naïvely trusting, but never satisfied; if they continually move the goalposts and seem more interested in finding 'a better way' than in delivering what they first promised.

Gridlock, if they lack vision, motivation and leadership; if they always find a reason not to act; and if they appear both weak and stubborn.

Radically new, if their processes are anarchic; if you never know who is in charge; if they take the participative style to extremes; if decisions take forever; if discussions about finance and value seem particularly difficult; if you find it hard to understand where they are coming from; and if it seems they are simply ignoring the contract between you.

Seeing others from arm's length

Partners in *arm's length* have reason to believe other partners are in:

Hearts and minds, if they are a little too 'pally' and you feel suffocated; and if you feel they do not approve of your procedures, but avoid confrontation.

Command and control, if they resist change; if they ignore your suggestions for improvements; if you see more or less eye to eye on risk management; if they insist on a 'plan'; if nothing happens, unless you get the approval of the right person; and if you become frustrated by their inflexibility.

Do and review, if they are always asking for more data; if their continuous improvement initiatives work well; if they are disappointed by your lack of creativity; and if you find it hard to trust them completely.

Gridlock, if their morale seems low and they have no sense of direction; if they obstruct more than they construct; and if they are apt to lose interest suddenly, for no apparent reason.

Radically new, if their processes are anarchic and they have no interest in 'best practice' or financial matters; if you are never sure you are talking to the 'right person'; and if they always want to discuss things with their colleagues, but act quickly and decisively as soon as agreement is reached.

Seeing others from do and review

Partners in *do and review* have reason to believe other partners are in:

Hearts and minds, if they hate your 'continuous improvement' programmes; if they insist on doing things their way; if they seem very people orientated; if they care more about values than processes, and if you like the way they are always looking for the creative solution.

Command and control, if they refuse to talk about improvement; if they seem secretive; if they get annoyed when proper procedures are flouted; if when things get difficult they ignore your solutions and slap the contract on the table; if they lack creativity; and if the person who makes the decisions is always too busy.

Arm's length, if you make good progress with processes at the interface; if they keep their distance; if they seem too defensive and if they emphasize their differences.

Gridlock, if their eyes glaze over if you start to talk about how processes could be improved; if they seem to lack motivation and leadership and seem blind to the opportunities; and if they don't implement your improvement ideas on the grounds that they are too risky.

Radically new, if it seems an exciting place to work; if there is plenty of creativity; and if they listen to you.

Seeing others from gridlock

When dealing with those in the left and middle columns of the grid, people in *gridlock* tend to feel powerless, frustrated and misunderstood, but may also suspect that, in their efforts to be understood, they are limiting the partnership's potential.

Partners in *gridlock* have reason to believe other partners are in:

Hearts and minds, if they appear intolerant of difference; if they seem too wedded to their 'vision'; if their power system is very centralized; and if, despite protestations about the need for participation, they seem unwilling to share power and always claim to have the right answer.

Command and control, if they seem too 'formal'; if they are unable to adapt to changed circumstances; if they keep going on about the 'contract'; and if they are sticklers for detailed plans and the 'right way'.

Arm's length, if they do not appear to trust you and play their cards close to their chests; and if they do not seem to be interested in your ideas.

Do and review, if they usually see things your way; if they are easy to get along with; if their emphasis is on incremental change; and if you feel they should trust you a little more than they seem to.

Radically new, if you begin to suspect you are your own worst enemy; and it is your defensiveness and lack of trust that is the real problem.

Seeing others when aiming at radically new

Partners who wish to move to *radically new* will have reason to believe they are dealing with partners in:

Hearts and minds, if they cannot tolerate difference; if they seem much too wedded to shared visions; if their power is centralized; and if they talk a lot about collaboration, but keep insisting their way is best.

Command and control, if they seem far too formal; if they cannot adapt well to new circumstances; and if they say the only way to get things done is to follow tried and tested procedures and abide by the letter of the contract.

Arm's length, if they do not seem to trust you quite enough; if they always play their cards close to their chests; and if they do not seem very open to new ideas.

Do and review, if they usually see things your way; if they are easy to get along with; if their focus is on 'incremental change'; and if you feel their people need to trust yours more to realize the full potential benefits of your partnership.

Gridlock, if they seem unadventurous; if they are attracted to your culture; and if they clearly find their own culture frustrating and dispiriting, but are reluctant to change it.

But, if the gridlocked organization's attempts to move to *radically new* are successful, its members will realize their perceptions were prejudices and will try to put them to one side. They will resist any temptation to induce their partners to change, because they will know that no single perception of what the partnership is or should be is correct. They will see the grid as a set of positions, all of which can be occupied by anyone or any organization at any time, depending on the context in which they find themselves.

Instead of trying to exhort and cajole their partners into different boxes on the grid, they will accept other positions as valid and look for common ground to act on, despite the differences.

Radically new is a strange place. Entering it is rather like entering a new dimension, where everything one has left behind is somehow preserved in the new outlook. We will explore it in more detail in the next four chapters.

The language of the grid

As the revelation people experience on entering *radically new* suggests, the journey we have just taken through the minds of people inhabiting the boxes of the grid has not produced accurate descriptions. It produces impressions and the only way to corroborate them is to ask the partner whether they are true. And the only way to treat the answers is to accept them as true, from the partner's point of view.

The value of the grid lies not in the precision of its descriptions or the truth it reveals, but in the language it provides for talk and conversation that can improve understanding.

In the next chapters, we will explore the language of the grid by looking at the new light it sheds on strategy, communication, leadership, trust and conflict.

Story from the front...

Use of symbols

When a major health services provider entered into a partnership by outsourcing facilities management, it was not looking for a solution to a short-term problem. The health services organization was looking for a style of partnership that could develop and find new ways of working together to the partners' mutual advantage.

Committed to this 'idea' of partnership, the service provider used the partnering grid to screen potential partners. From its own *do and review* plot, it found one prospective partner's *radically new* plot attractive, because it appeared to offer opportunities for improved services.

To build a better picture of where the two partners perceived themselves to be on the partnering grid, at an early meeting partner teams were asked to bring an object that symbolized how they thought of themselves. The facilities management team brought a condom to symbolize their vision of themselves as 'safe but exciting'.

Twelve months on, the partnership was reasonably successful, but had failed to achieve the degree of service enhancement first hoped for. Once more the parties gathered, artefacts in hand, to try to understand their failure to launch more innovative and profitable services. This time, the outsourcing partners brought a lemon to symbolize their feeling of 'being squeezed'. It was an inspired choice, because it made the health service provider realize that the facilities management organization had moved from its original, *radically new* position down the grid to *arm's length*.

Conversations matter more than grid mappings. The value lies not so much in knowing where you are as in talking about how you got there. Improving fit requires each side to understand the dynamics of the shift in perception so they can act together more effectively in future. The facilities management team felt that a year of being browbeaten by lawyers had forced them to abandon their ambitions and move to a cooler, *arm's length* relationship.

Changes in ownership and affiliation on both sides reduced the high initial level of trust and ideas that could have produced innovative services were not shared. The service provider's insistence on measuring their partner's performance in terms of inputs rather than outputs had made their partner unwilling to allocate resources for the improvement of service output and obliged it to concentrate on complying with increasingly accurate measurements of inputs.

During the anniversary meeting, the lemon concentrated minds wonderfully on the ways in which the partnership's processes and measurement systems might be changed to revive the partnership's original ambitions.

References

1. Is your strategic alliance really a sale?, J. Bleeke and D. Ernst, *HBR* Jan/Feb, 1995.
2. *Six Thinking Hats*, Edward de Bono (Little, Brown & Co., 1985).
3. *Organizational Learning: A Theory in Action Perspective*, C. Argyris and D. Schon (Addison-Wesley, 1978).

4

Living with difference

'The Map is not the Territory'
Alfred Korzybski, *Science and Sanity*

There has always been a trade-off between creativity and unity, but exactly where the balance should be struck changes as the nature of competition and the essence of competitive advantage change.

In their quest for creativity, organizations have become more trusting, made business units more autonomous and embraced the idea of 'empowerment'. The policies have worked in many cases, but before long the 'autonomous' businesses and 'empowered' people begin pursuing objectives different from, or in conflict with, the ambitions of the parent.

Dismayed by the loss of unity and a feeling that 'things are getting out of hand', many managers have decided the cost of the improvement in creativity has been too high and that autonomy and empowerment must be constrained in some way to restore lost unity. But then the pendulum swings too far the other way and the organization becomes locked in an endless oscillation as it seeks creativity through trust and unity through control. It seems that the more eagerly one is pursued, the more attractive the other becomes.

The fear of fragmentation, on the one hand, and the desire for creativity, on the other, have led some to believe that the secret is to empower business units and individuals to act on their own initiatives within the constraints of a strong culture and a unifying vision. Empowerment becomes a bargain between leader and led. 'You can have your freedom', says the leader 'if you declare your allegiance to my vision. You're not generally "empowered". You're only empowered to help me realize my dream.'

It is this conditional empowerment that creates the problem of 'buy-in'. If empowerment is to be limited, people must agree to its limitation and a lot of leadership effort must therefore be devoted to 'selling' the vision to those whose power it constrains.

This 'selling' process can be prolonged and frustrating and often leads to competitively disadvantageous delays in implementation. The usual response, however, is to seek faster, more effective 'selling' techniques, rather than to abandon the goal of an integrated view and recognize the multiplicity of individual agendas.

These strenuous efforts to achieve 'buy-in' are seldom successful. When the 'right' view must always be the leader's view, those who cannot or will not 'get with the programme' or who 'toe the line' instead of 'buying-in', are disenfranchised, feel disempowered and so behave in ways that frustrate the achievement of the leadership's objectives.

True empowerment ends when efforts to achieve buy-in begin. And the fault when buy-in is not achieved is held to be the individual's, not the leader's, because buy-in is an individual act of commitment.

Those who take a system's view of organizations say the failure to achieve buy-in is usually the result of a failure to understand the system. There is a lot to be said for the system's view of organizations, but we believe social systems such as business organizations are much too complex ever to be 'knowable' and that attempts to integrate different views into a single view are doomed to failure. They boil down to no more than an insistence that everyone must see the system the leader sees and help realize the leader's vision of what the system should become.

This is often a perfectly appropriate strategy, but there are certain times in certain industries – and, in many industries, the present is such a time – when creativity and flexibility are too important to risk destroying them by trying to impose unitary, 'official' versions of reality. These risks are particularly acute in partnerships because efforts to achieve cross-boundary buy-in amount to cultural colonization and the destruction of the very differences that drive the opportunities.

Multiple visions

Suppose for a moment that there is no objective reality and that what seems to you to be true is just one of many truths that could be seen by a group of people contemplating the same picture or strategic predicament.

You do not have to suspect your truth might be less true than the truths of others; you just have to try to imagine what it would be like to run, lead, or work within an organization where there is no objective truth and where your view of what is, and of what can or should be done, is no better (or worse) than anyone else's.

It could be objected that such total subjectivity is impossible, as demonstrated by the story of the six blind men who were asked to touch an elephant. The first man touched the leg and felt a tree, the second touched the tail and felt a rope, the third touched a rib and felt a wall, the fourth touched the trunk and felt a snake, the fifth touched a tusk and felt a branch, the sixth touched a toe and felt a stone. You need someone, it will be argued, to interpret and piece together the six impressions, to get to 'elephant'.

This kind of reasoning leads many organizations to constrain local freedoms for the sake of global visions and diligently to seek buy-in.

Hence the standard partnering story goes something like this.

Two very different organizations find they have to work together. Everyone knows that around 70% of such ventures fail and most assume it is because of the 'cultural differences'. Everyone also 'knows' that companies with similar cultures are slightly more successful. So, the problem is named and the solution clear – we need to make these two very different companies the same.

Quite apart from eroding the value that fueled the deal in the first place, this argument raises a whole new set of problems for our two companies.

All our people, they say, need to share the same vision, mission and values and we need to figure out how people need to behave if they are to fit into the new culture we are designing.

To get started, we'll get them together to share their aspirations with a view to getting buy-in and commitment to the new vision.

With help from a consultant, they cover the wall with sticky yellow notes declaring what it is they want to leave behind and what they want to take forward. Then lots of metrics are put in place to see how much progress everyone (else) is making.

In the meantime, people get on with daily action lists and business as usual and nothing remarkable happens. Many people feel that they're living in a vacuum. The most talented go elsewhere, many put all their energy into arguing about who's right or in control (often one and the same thing) and the rest become experts at keeping their heads down and their noses clean.

To counter this state of inertia, more solutions are designed and programmes are delivered as an antidote to the problem the last solution created.

Value seeps away like water into sand, shareholders call a halt and everyone gazes in dismay at the cost of disentanglement.

One territory, many maps

So is there is another way for the blind men to deduce the presence of an elephant? If we are bound by our promise to value every perception of reality equally, what can we do to help the blind men see?

First, we can recognize that when it comes to partnerships rather than elephants, we are all equally sighted and all equally blind. No one department, function, partner or manager has a picture of the partnership as it 'really is'.

Opportunities, threats, objectives and benefits move and change shape depending on the point from which we look at them. The search for a single immutable definition is the wrong solution to the wrong question.

Second, we could help them to develop a language to communicate with each other. Equipped with relevant knowledge, blind men can conceive of an elephant and, if they share a language, they can pool their impressions and work out what to do next.

Similarly, partners can share what they know, hear what others have to say, accept that there will be differences and treat the resulting picture as a very real part of the complexity in which they all operate.

This approach to handling difference is worth considering even by those who reject the idea of a 'subjective' reality. When it comes to making partnering work, the trouble with the alternative approach is that it assumes reality is objective and it is the leader's job to perceive it and to convince others that he or she is right.

Even if this were true, achieving buy-in is too difficult, costly and simply takes too long. If you must wait until everyone has been either persuaded or fired before you can act, you will probably be too late. It is better to acknowledge that people are different, to focus on what unites them, to map the 'common ground' that exists *now* and act on it right away.

When speed is of the essence, the only consensus that one can afford to wait for is the minimum consensus needed to act.

The primacy of action

Enterprises that act on common ground right away are faster, more agile and more responsive than enterprises that spend valuable time trying to get buy-in and they are different in other ways too.

They receive as well as transmit, because they are profoundly interested in the views and ambitions of all their members and devote their efforts not to changing people, but to changing the circumstances in which they relate to each other.

They may have strong leaders, but it is not a strength impatient with dissent. It is a strength that encourages other people to define their realities for themselves and provides processes to help them see and hear other points of view. The emphasis in such organizations is on relationships, not visions. People understand that their identities consist of their relationships and that what they can do and see is governed by the context in which they operate.

In the same way, collective action occurs when independent people recognize their inter-dependence and work out what they can do together. In this way, the paradox can be resolved and organizations can be diverse, empowered *and* united.

But it is not the kind of unity that comes from alignment of heart and mind and everyone 'singing from the same hymn sheet'. It is an adequate unity, a sufficiency of shared purpose, that accommodates individual purposes too.

This modest, but practical kind of shared purpose emerges from environments that allow everyone to contribute, learn from each other and see the common ground on which they can act together for their mutual benefit.

When a partnership in which power and knowledge are very widely distributed is nonetheless active and successful, we can assume that it has accumulated significant amounts of trust capital. But this is not the trust that comes from kinship ties or a shared culture. It is trust that emerges from common action, successfully undertaken.

Discovering the common ground

The dynamic of any organization is the dynamic of its 'common ground'; the place where individual dreams meet, negotiate a common future and agree to take steps towards it. If there is no common ground, or if it exists but is not discovered and mapped, there will be no common future and there will be calls for 'strong' leadership in the conventional sense.

To exploit the dynamics of the common ground, therefore, it is necessary to define it and to cultivate an atmosphere of mutual learning that allows the organization, and its members, to make sense of the past, to understand the present, to adapt to changes in context, to negotiate through dialogue and to act.

It is very difficult to cultivate such an atmosphere, however, because most people talk in private languages, such as technology, finance, marketing, production and personnel, that are more or less unintelligible to a non-specialist. A switch must be found to disconnect us from our familiar everyday discourses and force us to talk and negotiate in a language intelligible to everyone. Without such a language, the common ground where trust grows will remain patchy, infertile and largely invisible.

The partnering grid and the uncompromising straight talk it can generate gives us such a language and enables the partners to move the partnership to the strange extremity on the grid that we call *radically new*.

The following three chapters provide some indicators of what strategy, communications and leadership look like in this new territory.

5

Exploring common ground

Wealth is not gained by perfecting the known,
but by imperfectly seizing the unknown
Kevin Kelly, *New Rules for the New Economy*

At a concert in Athens, in front of a crowd of thousands, two violinists –
one white, one black; one male, one female – improvised a duet, while the
conductor and the rest of the orchestra looked on.

The music was marvellous; fast, precise and passionate, but was made
doubly exciting by the communication between the two musicians. Neither
spoke, but their eyes and expressions, and the rhythmic swaying of their
bodies, were eloquent testimony to the richness of their conversation. As
the initiative switched from one to the other, according to a cueing system
invisible to all but themselves, the audience could see them challenging
each other to outdo the other's virtuosity and inventiveness with new and
ever wilder variations. She began plucking and he took up the pizzicato with
no audible break; he began to bow faster and higher and then it was she
playing faster and higher still.

At times they seemed to co-operate and at times they seemed to compete.
The warmth of the looks they exchanged suggested that they were sharing a
peak experience and knew that the music they were making was better than
either could have made on their own.

At the end, the applause was rapturous.[1]

The duet could have been recorded, transcribed and performed again, but
the act of its creation was spontaneous. It was not an expression of a score or
of a conductor's interpretation – it 'emerged' from a space consisting of
a stage, a common professional expertise, a love of music and the violin, a

mutual respect for and faith in each other's skill and musical instinct, and a shared wish to create something extraordinary that their fellow musicians would admire and their audience would applaud.

They did not know what it would turn out like before they started, but they knew the space was full of opportunity and they would not get such a chance again to transcend themselves before an audience in the shadow of the Parthenon.

The poverty of intentional strategy

The trouble with a conventional strategy is that it is a plan and when the environment is changing fast, plans can become prisons. When the enterprise is a partnership, plans can become liabilities because the exercise of control needed to embark on them and keep them on track can destroy the joint enterprise.

Some say that although the volatility of today's business environment means that strategy has to be flexible, all enterprises (including partnerships) need general strategic guidelines, because without a sense of direction the enterprise will wander around aimlessly, achieving nothing.

It is true that clarity of purpose and intent is essential, but strategic guidelines are not its only conceivable source. It is already implicit in the decision to form a partnership, because that is inspired by the anticipation of some joint benefit and its development emerges thereafter as all the overlapping perceptions, ambitions, abilities and imaginations of the partners interact in the partnership space.

The violinists at the Acropolis lacked even a rudimentary score. Their plan was merely to improvise. Their sense of direction came from themselves and the setting; from where they were, who they were, what they could do, their knowledge of each other's personality and talent and their determination to make good use of the opportunity they had to display their art. Each phrase created adjacent possibilities for subsequent phrases.

It is just the same in fast-moving businesses. Action is not a static, long-term plan you carry with you; it is a thought for the day that has emerged from what happened yesterday and will more than likely be replaced by an enhanced thought tomorrow.

This does not mean the abandonment of core purpose in pursuit of an ever changing array of management approaches and strategies. It means holding tightly onto core purpose while remaining flexible and open to changes in the means of achieving it.

If by 'strategy' one means deliberate intent embedded in detailed long-term plans, then strategy is very close to its sell by date. There is a need for a more humble kind of short-term project planning in a partnership, but the deliberate fixed plan associated with the word 'strategy' is replaced by a searching process – an exploration of adjacent possibilities created by actions taken in the partnership space.

It is the same in conventional business. What management theorists proclaim as inspired strategies, brilliantly implemented, usually turn out on closer inspection to be the results of cleverly exploiting lucky accidents or chance encounters. Many of the textbook cases of brilliant business strategies of recent years are *ex-post* explanations that only seem to be 'intentional' in retrospect. The well-known case of Honda's entry into the US market (Honda intended to sell big motorcycles, but Americans were more interested in the mopeds its staff used) illustrates the role of serendipity and emergence in the successes of ostensibly intentional 'strategies'.

Strategy and the grid

The grid in strategic mode is shown in Figure 5.1. Its six boxes map the six perceptions of partnership as follows:

Perception of partnership	*Perception of strategy*
Command and control	Plan
Hearts and minds	Vision
Arm's length	Protocol
Do and review	Process
Gridlock	Consensus
Radically new	Granular

Let's look at these six boxes in a little more detail.

Bottom left

In *command and control*, a strategy is a long-term intent that takes precedence over everything and everyone. The future has a special status here

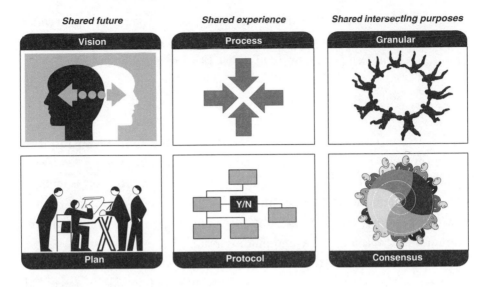

Figure 5.1 *Strategy grid*

and is assumed to be malleable. It is encapsulated in written plans of great perceived potency. There is usually a strategic plan, drafted by an individual or a small planning group and an implementation plan drafted later. Predictability and control are both seen as essential qualities of the planning process and it is taken for granted that a faithful implementation of the plan will bring about the desired outcomes.

Consider the case of a large engineering firm which formed a small team to look ahead and suggest ways in which it could maximize its survival chances in an increasingly competitive market.

One of the main ideas to emerge was a major re-structuring of the company, involving many new lines of interaction between individuals and teams and thus the formation of a host of new internal and external relationships or partnerships. The team spent six months shut away in a Portakabin gathering data and dreaming up ideas. The analysis was exemplary, the problems were well understood, the detail was precisely documented, but the ideas were the ideas of engineers – elegant, precise, low tolerance. They took no account at all of the fact that their application would substantially change the working lives of a large number of people. People were seen as components.

When this was pointed out by someone from a different part of the company, the planners realized they had more work to do. Rather than gathering information from the hitherto neglected components, however, they set about planning how to implement their plan. Eight months into the project most employees were unaware of its existence.

Top left

In *hearts and minds*, the 'strategic intent' takes the form of an inspiring vision and the focus remains firmly on a shared future. Strategy formation remains the responsibility of top management, but far more effort is made to win the commitment of those affected by it. Written documents are important here too, but they take the form not of plans, but of visions and statements of mission, value and guiding principles.

In addition, leaders often embark on company-wide roadshows consisting of presentations, question and answer sessions and so-called 'town hall meetings' at every site, to spread the gospel of the new vision and urge people to exert themselves in its pursuit. The 'envisioning' process relies heavily on will and intention and the implementation process is seen as a matter of doing what is needed to get from 'as is' to 'to be' states.

The leaders of one large multinational decided that their vision of the future could only be realized if everyone subscribed to and always acted in accordance with five 'core values'. Much time and considerable sums in consultancy fees were spent on selecting and drafting the values, which were then printed on small plastic cards and issued to employees. Thousands of larger copies were also made and distributed for public display.

One of the authors was walking through the company's accounts department when she spotted a 'core value' poster stuck up on a wall, next to the photocopier. The third core value was 'We respect each other' but someone had crossed out the first two letters of the second word and replaced them with 'su'. There is always another view.

Bottom middle

In *arm's length* the past is more important, because it is the source of the shared experiences from which partners derive their rules of interaction, or protocols. The emphasis is not on where they are going, but on the way they take each step.

Clear norms of interaction are established and much effort is devoted to scanning the environment for information about how to improve the quality of interactions within the established norms. Strategic plans and implementation programmes usually take the form of a sequence of steps or phases.

A consortium of service organizations had come together to deliver a long-term contract into the public sector. Member firms were struggling with issues of trust and coherence of actions taken by various partner companies. They decided that the best way to solve these issues was to be specific about *how* the consortium partners acted, rather than to discuss what they were doing and why.

Over a period of several months, a joint team worked hard to produce a joint operating manual that documented in great detail every possible management and resource process relevant to the consortium. Rules and protocols were clearly stipulated and disseminated to all consortium members. Unfortunately, the size of the manual was such that few if any consortium members read or referred to it and, ultimately, it was abandoned in favour of a simple list of ten operating principles that all could see and understand. In the language of the grid, a shift had taken place from *arm's length* towards *hearts and minds*.

Top middle

Shared experiences are also the inspiration of strategy in *do and review*, but in this case, the partnering protocols become processes that are always under review. As in *arm's length*, the future and 'strategy' are less important than what can be learned from what has already happened.

Past experience is the inspiration of strategy here too, but strategic 'input' is gathered more widely, particularly from front-line or 'customer-facing' staff and efforts are made to achieve a broader alignment of objectives to ensure that the relationship continues after current projects are completed.

There is a sense in this box that the partnership itself has 'a right to life' and thus possesses its own strategic momentum.

After a consultancy had completed a major systems project for a specialist retailer, it felt that it had learned quite a bit about its client's business. So the consultants' project team asked for a meeting with the client's CEO to discuss other possibilities.

As a result of that and subsequent meetings at various levels of the two organizations, a joint venture company was formed to offer the solution to non-competing retailers with similar system requirements.

The joint venture already has two satisfied clients and talks are now in progress on extending its range of services.

Bottom right

In *gridlock*, strategy becomes fuzzier and action is informed by mutual understanding – or, rather, inhibited by the lack of it.

The present looms larger than the past or the future because it is accepted that the destinies of the partners are linked and all that is left is to decide what to do next within the common ground that has been mapped out. Strategy emerges as a series of projects, from regular meetings, and much effort is devoted to ensuring that there is something for everyone.

But areas of potential difficulty or friction are avoided, so they tend to grow until the partnership becomes trapped in a state of inertia, where survival becomes the main objective.

A 'Future Search' conference[2] was held bringing together a diverse cross-section of stakeholders in order to encourage positive change in a large industrial city in the north of England. The process enables people with different stakes in a common task to explore their shared past, map their current context, explore possible futures and plant action flags on common ground. It emphasizes what is doable now over what might be possible if only people could be changed.

Eight groups of eight people, each reflecting a different stake in the overall task of working towards a better future for the city, shared their perceptions, dreams and differences. These stakeholder groups representing areas such as education, youth, business and health were able to see and hear where their differences were keeping them apart and disabling them from building bridges together.

The potential breakthrough to a *radically new* partnership was in their sights and a great deal of energy, enthusiasm and commitment filled the room.

At the end of the conference when public commitments to action are made, people self-managed their action priorities and the groups who would work together to see them through. And it was here that an old tendency to *gridlock* re-appeared.

Steeped still in historical divisions and political agendas, many people drifted away from the new allegiances they had made during the future search and stuck to comfortable and familiar ground with the people with whom they had always worked. Some exciting and innovative projects emerged and certainly people believed in some different possibilities. That said, however, the risks were too great and the divides too great to break away and work with the politically risky.

Top right

In *radically new*, partners understand that what matters is not how well they understand each other, but what they are already willing and able to do. The present dominates both right-hand boxes but in *radically new*, much greater efforts are made to understand and map the common ground from which 'doable' projects emerge.

Continual updating of information about the environment, and about the widest possible range of individual aspirations, is a distinctive feature of such relationships. The strategy is not 'intended'; it emerges from the projects that materialize from the wide-ranging conversations among the constantly expanding partnership community.

At the time of writing we are setting up a new joint research project, with a group of partner organizations, to explore in more depth some of the issues raised by our work to date.

In view of the vital role played by the distribution of power in determining the nature and creativity of relationships, all the members have chosen to abandon traditional ownership. Instead, the whole group has co-designed activities in such a way that power, knowledge, purpose and thus any value created are also distributed.

In the first working meeting with the core members, the issue of strategy in distributed communities was discussed at some length, thereby providing the space to address the group's survival and sustainability. This is not as straightforward as it might seem because conversations are always started by an individual. This inevitably 'positions' the initiator as a proposer and obliges other members of the group to respond to the proposal, either by rejecting it or buying in to it.

There was an almost palpable shift of emphasis, from buy-in to collaboration, when we all faced the fact that survival was not guaranteed and that it was up to us to work together, to give it life.

A strong sense of commitment emerged from this meeting, which we attributed to the group's success in mapping out patterns of current and future conversations, which would keep all our separate ideas and actions inter-related in a 'collaborative' space.

The conventional buy-in model would have led us down a safe and predictable path. The model we have chosen has opened up 'common ground' that is already alive with a host of possible projects and alliances, from knowledge creation to commercial applications, the complexity and richness of which could not have been seen, let alone explored and co-ordinated, had the partnership been 'managed' from a single perspective.

Emergent strategy

In a *radically new* partnership, strategy development 'emerges' from a series of projects that create possibilities for subsequent projects. When a partnership space is rich, it can produce something so good and so in tune with the times, it seems afterwards as if it must have been planned. Exploiting such opportunity, as Henry Mintzberg reminds us, is not a question of deliberate planning, but of crafting a path idea by idea, step by step, and working with what emerges.[3]

All enterprises need some stability to prevent them from falling apart, but because stability threatens agility, the stabilizing elements of the system are always being challenged. Most organizations are battlegrounds where the official and the formal are constantly fighting with the unorthodox and the subversive. In traditional integrated organizations, there is enough central power to keep subversives at bay. But *radically new* partnerships lack central power. They are more open to challenge, more vulnerable to subversive conspiracies and, therefore, less stable.

Most people see this instability as a weakness, but it is unavoidable in a partnership where difference is valued and can be a great strength in turbulent environments where adaptability and creativity are vital. Ralph Stacey[4] has argued that it is only when an organization is stable and unstable *at the same time* that it can generate new forms of behaviour and innovate. He says the creative process 'is inevitably messy' and 'to remove the mess, by inspiring us to follow some common vision, share the same culture, and pull together, is to remove...the raw material of creative activity'.

But the fact that *radically new* partnerships cannot be 'controlled' does not doom them to anarchy. The sense of shared destiny and the 'common ground' that initially inspired the partnership serve to contain the instability and provide the context for 'emergent' strategy. Stacey suggests that the human need to belong and 'sustain the support of others is a very powerful form of control', but it is exerted not by a leader, because there is no leader, but by the group as a whole. As Stacey put it: 'There is control, but no one is "in control".'

Radically new partnerships are good examples of the complex adaptive systems studied by complexity scientists. Although on the edge of chaos, they display ordered patterns of behaviour, the detailed consequences of which are unpredictable but which can nonetheless be relied on to maintain a partnership's balance on the edge of collapse.

Structure as strategy

As more and more companies feel obliged to join partnerships in which power is more widely distributed than they are used to, the shapes of enterprises become more fluid and changeable, action is more spontaneous and harder to direct and strategic decision making becomes more difficult. One could say that in conventional partnerships, strenuous and largely successful efforts are made to emulate the tightness of conventional enterprise architectures, but that in the new, more democratic partnerships required in, and becoming characteristic of e-business, for instance, novel enterprise structures are emerging that achieve the constrained instability that fosters creativity.

Some say structure *is* strategy and competition consists not, as is usually supposed, of a *strategic* but of a *structural* arms race, in which different enterprise structures are endlessly trying to achieve creativity advantages over their rivals. Some years ago, Gianni Lorenzoni and Charles Baden-Fuller suggested that one of the most striking developments in business during the early 1990s had been the emergence of what they called 'tight networks' as competitors to conventional integrated enterprises.[5]

The roles they gave to the 'central firm' in such networks, and the emphasis they placed on shared visions and cultural compatibility, suggest the tight network model is not well suited to today's more chaotic environ-ments, but we believe much of what Lorenzoni and Baden-Fuller said remains relevant to modern business partnerships. Their 'central firms', for example, relied on non-contractual means to bind the networks to-gether, because they knew that formal contracts covering every eventuality reduced flexibility and eroded the network's cost advantage. They also used their power with care, because they realized that if they used it in arbitrary, self-serving ways, the network could disintegrate.

The democratic nature of tight networks is reflected in the distribution of economic value. Many McDonald's and Benetton franchisees, for example, earn higher returns on capital than their central firms and private infor-mation is anathema; members routinely exchange data, ideas or hunches about market trends. Nike invites its partners to its Beaverton research laboratory to show them new developments in materials, design, technology and markets and Toyota sub-contractors receive training from the central firm. Structure also affects the quality of information. Within a hierarch-ical, integrated structure, knowledge is often treated as an attribute of power and tends to be transmuted as it is transmitted. In tight networks knowledge is a common resource. It flows more freely, widely and transparently, with greater frequency and more impact on decision making.

But Lorenzoni and Baden-Fuller say it is hard to develop a true infor-mation-sharing culture. They found a number of cases in which the alliance failed because partners abused their information-sharing privileges. In one case, a delinquent member used valuable network information as an entry ticket to a rival alliance. It is thus risky for a member of a tight network to be open with information and it will be reluctant to take the risk in the absence of trust and a commitment to reciprocity.

The need for trust stems from the 'tightness' of the network; from the idea that the partnership is permanent and that long-term commitments are needed to make it work. In the kind of partnerships emerging in e-business, trust is not a pre-condition because although the relationship may last for some time, the environment is so volatile partners must assume it will not last beyond the completion of the project at hand. Trust is a pre-requisite in a tight network because without it very little can be done, but in the more opportunistic partnerships suited to volatile environments, it is a quality that grows as it is earned. It is not some grand transcendent ethos, based on a joint commitment to a shared vision, because there is no shared vision in such partnerships. It is a more humble, practical quality that improves the effectiveness of communication and helps to extend the common ground.

In this kind of partnership there is no permanent central firm. A member of the partnership who takes the lead in one project, or project stage, will be happy to play a supporting role in the next. The centre moves to the member best equipped to lead the work at hand.

The impetus to undertake particular projects emerges from the common ground and that frisson of anxiety that runs through organizations balanced on the edge of instability. If people are anxious, but self-confident, and if they respect the abilities of their partners, they will want to find more things to do together.

What they can do together (the partnership's opportunity set) is determined by the adjacent possibilities revealed by what they have done already and who they are. The complete opportunity set is defined by the 'hinterlands' of the partners, that is their backgrounds (and baggage) which are comprised of the experiences, skills, networks and ambitions they bring with them. But the portion of the opportunity set that is accessible depends on the connections between these hinterlands. In other words, the more members learn about the abilities, networks and dreams of their partners, the more opportunities they will see and the more energetic, creative and adaptable the partnership will become.

There is 'intention' in this interplay between hinterlands, but only in the form of the dreams and aspirations of individuals. 'Strategy' is a personal thing and *radically new* partnership 'strategy' emerges from a cross-fertilisation of personal life plans. The partnership acts because each member believes the agreed step will further his or her intention. It is like the violin duet – the partnership setting requires action, but no one is absolutely sure where that action will lead.

Emergent structure

An important aspect of the virtuous instability of a *radically new* partnership enterprise is that its structure is as 'emergent' as its strategy. Membership of the enterprise changes constantly as it re-configures itself for each project. Partners come, go and come back again. There is no 'tenure' and thus very little inertia.

Speed in forming working relationships and ending them without damaging the personal relationships that will facilitate a resumption at some later date contributes to the exceptional adaptability which is one of a partnership's competitive advantages in times of rapid and unpredictable change.

This emergent structure facilitates the emergence of strategy by making it easier to correct enterprise direction 'on the run'. The main weakness of a conventionally formulated strategy in a turbulent environment is that it is equivalent to aiming a cannon at a moving target. When strategy and structure are provisional and subject to change in the light of changed circumstances, the cannon is exchanged for a guided missile capable of following the target's twists and turns.

We will discuss how this 'emergent' nature of strategy requires a different approach to information sharing and different kinds of conversation in the next chapter. We will end this chapter by providing a real life example of a *radically new* enterprise: ARM.

ARM's way: partnering in multiple dimensions

When Cambridge-based Acorn Computers decided to spin out its microprocessor design team in November 1990, forming Advanced RISC Machines (ARM), the new company was faced with a strategic dilemma.

Five years earlier, the part of Acorn that is now ARM had designed the first commercial, single-chip RISC (Reduced Instruction Set Computer) processor.

From the beginning, ARM processors were designed to deliver high performance at low cost. It soon became apparent to the ARM team, however, that the low power consumption of RISC chips, which meant longer battery life and cooler running, was an equally important quality and they optimized later designs for energy efficiency.

The dilemma was the mismatch between ARM's limited resources and the huge market for small, fast, energy-efficient chips that were easy to program and had very good 'code density' (they need less memory than competing RISC chips and so reduce system costs).

The traditional way to exploit such a lead in semiconductors is to raise a pile of money and become an integrated design, development, manufacturing and marketing company.

When Robin Saxby was interviewed for the job of ARM's first CEO, he proposed a different approach.

'We started with £1.75 m and Acorn's intellectual property', Saxby told us in 1996. 'My idea was to run very lean and very quickly and to get into profit fast. We had outstanding people, a leading architecture and the chance to transform it from an Acorn into a global standard – but we didn't have the capital for manufacturing.'

Partnership was central to Saxby's plan. He saw ARM's essence as the design and development of RISC processors and systems and was determined to stick to that. Everything else needed to turn ARM chips into world beaters, such as software, software tools, systems building, manufacturing, marketing and distribution, would be provided through a policy Saxby calls 'partnering in multiple dimensions'.

ARM did not come to partnering. It was built on it. 'That is the benefit of a clean sheet of paper,' Saxby said. 'We had no history so we could plan for a global partnership from the outset, and concentrate on doing what we were best at.'

The shape of ARM's global partnership was sculpted by its initial investors and the market segments for which its products were best suited. The three 'trade investors' (Acorn, Apple and VLSI) were also ARM partners, but did not have exclusive rights to ARM technology. Between 1990, when VLSI took the first licence, and the end of 2001, ARM issued licences to 37 companies. 'We can license to anyone we want,' explained Saxby. 'We charge an up-front fee, and then a royalty per piece.'

The chances are high that the person reading these words right now will use a device controlled by an ARM chip some time today. ARM chips are literally everywhere. They control Nokia and many other mobile phones, PDAs (personal digital assistants), network computers, set-top boxes, digital televisions and are embedded in cars, Nintendo GameBoys, many other games consoles, printers, disk drives, fax machines, modems, network controllers and video sub-systems. In 2001 ARM chip designs accounted for over three-quarters of the world's 32-bit embedded RISC microprocessor market.

An important non-technical attraction for consumer goods manufacturers (the 'embedded' market) is that ARM's multiple partnerships make it easier for them to arrange local sources of supply. Structure is also strategy.

Having identified the key market segments, ARM developed and published what Saxby calls 'roadmaps' – product development plans that were

made available to licensees, so they could design their own product development strategies around specifications for the more advanced chips that
ARM had committed itself to developing.

These 'roadmaps' exemplify ARM's partnering philosophy because they
reveal vital product development information to partners that would be
regarded as highly confidential in a conventional company. Saxby saw it
differently. He wanted ARM partners to commit long term to the ARM
architecture and, to be willing to do that, they had to know what ARM had
up its sleeve. 'It costs us, and our semiconductor partners, several million
dollars to develop a new chip,' he said, 'so we have to be sure there are
products ready and waiting for it. The network is a model of openness, as
well as of partnership.'

Partnership characterizes ARM's research and development too. It spends
30 % of sales on R&D, often in partnership with universities and other
research establishments. As Saxby put it 'we re-cycle intellectual property'.
ARM is part of the 'Cambridge keiretsu', the affiliation of friends that
spawned its parent, Acorn, and scores of other high-tech companies that
have sprung up around the city.

At the other end of the value chain, ARM reserves the right, in its
licence agreements, to 'see through' its semiconductor partners and deal
with their customers directly. There is an evangelical aspect to selling
something new and the best evangelists are those who are wedded to the
faith and know the roadmaps. 'We are the keepers of the ARM architecture', Saxby explained. 'We must take charge of the main marketing thrust,
because our partners are more interested in promoting themselves.'

ARM and a semiconductor partner will often act as a marketing team to
open up new markets. Saxby said that with the help of its partnership
model, ARM could penetrate a new market in two years. 'Partnership allows
rapid market acceptance,' Saxby said, 'creates open, global standards and,
because of the wider geographical spread it provides, it makes you much less
vulnerable to local economic volatility.'

'It seems to work, in the early stages at least', Saxby told us in 1996.
'We are self-funding, and cash generating.' Sales had risen from less
than £1 m in 1991 to £10 m in 1995 and, after losses of £2 m in the
first two years, the operating profit had topped the £3 m mark. As a
growth strategy, it remained unproven, but Saxby seemed confident that
teamwork, networking, joint sales activity, constant innovation and acqui-

sitions of complementary technology and people would keep the momentum going.

They did. ARM was successfully floated in 1998. It announced revenues of over £146 m and pre-tax profits of over £50 m for 2001, even amid extremely difficult trading conditions. At the time of writing, tech stocks have again been hit hard, and ARM is no exception. But respectable profitability and a cash pile of £122m when others in the sector are in freefall provide a powerful testament to the inherent strength of ARM's partnering approach.

'We didn't set out to change the past,' said Saxby (who was 'Sir' Robin by now). 'We set out to do something for the future. We had to do things differently if we were going to become world class.'

A new enterprise model

ARM's 'strategy,' if one can call it that, is more a creature of the firm's nightmares than of its dreams. It did not want to manufacture, it did not relish going back, cap in hand, to investors for more cash all the time and diluting employees' equity and, above all, it did not want to be gobbled up by a large, bureaucratic organization that would stifle its creativity and subject its R&D budget to the mercies of across-the-board cost cuts.

ARM 'borrows' its strategy from its partners. It is a vital node in several enterprises competing in several markets, but its ultimate fate is in the hands of the customers of those software developers, systems designers and chip makers who are its partners. It takes pains to explore and understand the hinterlands of all its partners, particularly their customers, and it makes strenuous efforts to communicate on as broad a bandwidth as possible.

It is of no consequence whether or not ARM's partners see their own business relationships – including those with ARM – in the same way. ARM is happy to work with and adapt to any organization whose interests and competences are complementary with its own. It selects partners with great care, but not on the basis of similarity. It is difference that ARM values most in partners, because the more different partners are, the more they will widen ARM's own opportunities.

ARM's notion of partnership is also evident in its openness (exemplified by its 'roadmaps') and in the democratic nature of its partnerships. It is not in awe of, or overpowered by, its much larger partners. There are times and situations in which it plays supporting roles, but there are also occasions when its know-how makes it the natural project leader.

Although it has been promiscuous in its partnering so far, it is loyal, and regards each relationship as potentially long term. It cannot predict where the relationship will lead; it is content to take one step at a time in the belief that the more the relationship is explored, the more opportunities will emerge. Its people are poly-cultural, alert, highly communicative and responsive and insatiably curious about the hinterlands of the people they deal with. They are ready to take risks but they question everything, are no respecters of authority and are hungry for success in joint enterprises where rewards are shared in ways that seem to them to be fair.

They are inspired not by a specific business vision but by a faith in the RISC technology they have mastered, and of which they are the 'keepers', as Sir Robin put it. They will go where it leads; they do not want to plan its life in detail. They are great project planners, but have no 'strategy' in the conventional sense, apart from a wish not to miss good opportunities or make mistakes twice and a resolve to maintain their balance in the rapidly changing business environment.

References

1. On video: *Yanni Live at the Acropolis* with the Royal Philharmonic Concert Orchestra (Private Music, 1994).
2. *Future Search. An Action Guide to Finding Common Ground in Organizations and Communities*, M.R. Weisbord and S. Janoff (Berrett-Koehler, 1995).
3. *Mintzberg on Management*, H. Mintzberg (Free Press, 1989).
4. *Complexity and Creativity in Organizations*, R. Stacey (Berrett-Koehler, 1996).
5. *Creating a strategic centre to manage a web of partners*, G. Lorenzoni and C. Baden-Fuller, *California Management Review*, Spring, 1995.

6

Trading in 'common' sense

*Good breeding consists in concealing how
much we think of ourselves and how little we
think of the other person*

Mark Twain, *Notebooks*

A central feature of *radically new* is a transparent philosophy of communications which pervades every conversation from the informal chat around the coffee machine to the formal quarterly review. The reason we need a fresh approach to communication is that our conventional philosophy offers no way of helping partners transcend the 'power games' and 'hidden agendas' which prevent the really important matters from being discussed.

Take Bernard Shaw's exchange between Napoleon and Guiseppe:[1]

> *Napoleon*: What shall I do with this soldier Guiseppe? Everything he says is wrong.
> *Guiseppe*: Make him a general, excellency, and then everything he says will be right.

Guiseppe was describing an attitude to knowledge that is just as common today as it was in Napoleon's time. Because we can never know 'the whole truth', we attribute veracity to views, descriptions, statements and observations according to the pedigree of the source.

There is so much information around these days that we have to delegate the task of reducing it to digestible pieces to newspaper and TV editors. And it is not just broadcast media that are affected in this way. Face-to-face conversations and, in particular, business and work meetings, mediated as they are by politics, prejudice, individual interests, false assumptions and unwarranted inferences, are woefully inefficient and ineffective.

But what can we do to make business talk more efficient and effective?

To answer this question we need to look first at what we mean by knowledge and to follow that by a much closer look at how we use language.

Knowledge at work

The first thing we must do is to recognize that our understanding of knowledge is not what it was. In the past, we believed that most of what was known could be known 'for sure' in a scientific way. Now it is more common to accept that a growing amount of what presents itself as truth is not really truth at all, but opinion and point of view. Although some of what we do in business can still be based on facts, more and more of our decisions, such as whether or not to invest our money in Enron or World-Com, must be based on information that is inherently equivocal.

The value of knowledge is influenced by time, place, function, culture and the personal agendas of people with the power to make their views and judgments official.

It is not practical or even possible to get at the 'real truth' or to 'cleanse' conversations of their contaminants, but it is possible to get more of the situation, the assumptions and even the 'hidden agendas' out into the open. After all, it is these tacit, almost hidden rules about how we talk to each other which determine how we get work done. When we speak, we not only trade in words, we also trade our knowledge, the power we have to make things happen and, as a result, the meaning we build and share together. And it is this shared framework which determines what we can and cannot do.

Figure 6.1 shows interactions between people from different perspectives on the grid as forms of trade in power, knowledge and meaning.

On the left of the grid, where power and knowledge are concentrated, people trade power according to rules of interaction that are either explicit and taken for granted, in the case of *command and control*, or are embedded and largely hidden in the culture, in the case of *hearts and minds*.

In the middle of the grid, where power is still concentrated but knowledge is spread more widely, the knowledge trade is managed in the interests of process improvement in *arm's length*, or in ways that encourage people to participate in developing the partnership in *do and review*.

In both cases, knowledge is seen as a commodity; a common resource that can be accumulated, processed, organized and managed centrally. This

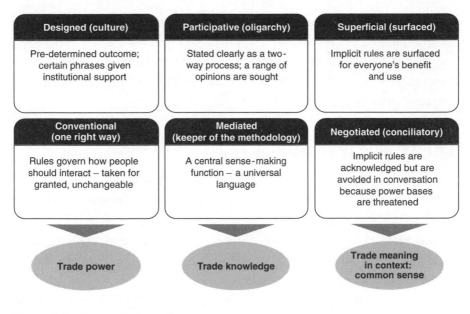

Figure 6.1 *Communication grid*

approach to communications has been embedded in the 'knowledge management' systems built by companies to store the organization's knowledge in knowledge bases accessible to all.

In some cases only certain people are allowed to build knowledge bases. There may also be strict definitions of what kind of knowledge is worthy of inclusion in the central archive. These rules tend to be less strict in *do and review* and people are encouraged to contribute to and make use of their knowledge, provided it falls within the framework set by the leadership.

On the right of the grid, knowledge ceases to be a mere commodity and comes to be seen as the source of 'common' sense through common sense *making*. There are rules, of course, but they are made visible to all and all can contribute to modifying or repealing them. Sense making is no longer confined to monarchs and oligarchs – it becomes a collective endeavour.

In *gridlock*, some of the rules remain sacrosanct and inhibit action, but in *radically new* all rules are out in the open and negotiable. There are no high-level languages of organizational aspiration – just a desire to act on the common ground revealed when people share meaning.

Generally speaking, one can say the rules of interaction become more visible as one moves from left to right across the grid, more voices are heard and conversation has less to do with planning and predetermined destination.

But it is one thing to acknowledge that partnerships have to 'act on common ground' and quite another to know how to inspire the sorts of conversation which reveal it.

The importance of dialogue

According to research into corporate re-structuring by A.T. Kearney and leading European business school IMD,[2] by far the most common method of achieving change is to replace the senior management team. The study showed that 75% of the top performing companies had changed their management before re-structuring and only 32% of the rest of the sample of 211 responses had undergone such change.

We do not believe this rite of management sacrifice (often at the behest of disenchanted investors) is the only or even the best way to achieve change. Our research suggests the 'changeability' of a business, whether integrated enterprise or partnership, has more to do with its style of inter-action and communication than with the competence or otherwise of its senior managers. Management sacrifices only become necessary when other ways of 'unblocking' the organization's communication flows have either not worked or, more often, not even been attempted.

We aim to show in this chapter how the *radically new* approach to partnering has implications for communication conventions in all enter-prises, not just partnerships. It is not easy, because it requires new power structures, a new language and a style of interaction which those with power to lose may, at first, find unsettling.

But if the alternative for leaders of traditional organizations is ritual sacrifice, they may feel the approach outlined here is worth considering. As for partnerships, we believe these techniques, principles and frameworks are vital to success.

In the typical, 'single-voice' style of business conversation, senior managers use their power (usually unconsciously) to control meaning, belief and action. We are not suggesting that they should surrender their power or abdicate their leadership responsibilities. We are saying that they must be more conscious of the effect of their power and should use it, not to control and direct meaning, but to create the conditions where many voices can be heard.

Only when there is a space for collective interpretation can all the different views come together and produce some 'common' sense. Dialogue, in this sense, is made possible not by individual skill but when a conversational space is deliberately designed so that a different kind of talk can lead to a different kind of action.[3]

We believe that, in a complex, fast-changing world where opportunities are fleeting and easily missed and emerging threats are hard to spot, the habit of dialogue within integrated *and* partnership-based enterprises can be an enormous competitive advantage.

Every conversation takes place within a context. Dialogue makes the context part of the conversation. It is an essential form of communication for a *radically new* partnership because the only way to achieve the mutually satisfactory outcomes partnerships seek is to hear what others are saying and sense what others are feeling, before deciding what to do together.

From monologue to dialogue

A senior departmental manager of a multinational engineering group called a meeting of his staff to discuss empowering them to take continuous improvement initiatives. That, at any rate, was the public agenda for the meeting. The manager's other objective was to solicit views about why things did not seem to be working very well.

Participants were asked to say how satisfied they were with the company, in relation to the characteristics of a 'learning company'.[4]

On the whole, the meeting seemed to go well, although only the more confident staff members felt able to speak out in such a large group. There were some interesting discussions, including one about the usefulness or otherwise of the reward system. One member of staff felt that the reward system could be reviewed and suggested some rather vague ideas about what could be done to improve it.

The manager listened patiently to the criticisms of the existing system for a time, but when the conversation turned to people's experiences with other systems, he closed the conversation down by listing the problems a change would cause, so preventing further suggestions. In so doing, rather than really hear the story from a different perspective, he maintained a sort of monologue. A working dialogue, by way of contrast, would have created space for these differences to be heard out.

Dialogue has become a hot management topic, but much of the literature (see Dixon[5] for a good summary) elevates it to the status of an art form. If dialogue is a pure, untainted, 'authentic' kind of conversation, which can only occur between those initiated in its secrets, it becomes exclusive and of little practical use.

Our approach is both more modest *and* more ambitious: more modest in that we see working dialogue as an occasional event that does not require special training or an elite cadre of (expensive) facilitators to manage it and more ambitious in that we believe everyone, or as many interested parties as possible, should be involved.

Sending people on courses to learn the habits and principles of dialogue is helpful, but it is the outcome of a dialogue that matters, not the process. Conversations can never be wholly cleansed of power, prejudice and personal agendas. The important thing is to provide a space for talk in which power, prejudice and personal agendas are part of what people can discuss rather than just the hidden framework within which the talk takes place.

Dialogue is not a warm, cosy activity. The sort of uncompromising straight talk we refer to obliges people to abide by certain rules that can be hard and even painful to follow. But because the rules do not have to be learned beforehand and require no prior practice, no one has to learn to *be* different before they can take part. Provided the principles are built into the structure of the conversation itself, anyone can do it and do it right away.

Principles of working dialogue

Rules are necessary in *radically new* conversations. Dialogue is not a natural style of interaction for people who are more used to the sort of organizational talk where much, if not most, is left unsaid.

Readers who decide to design spaces for working dialogue should not do so without first examining the principles with which they intend to work. Here are some of the most important principles to keep in mind:

1. *Make it matter.* The agenda should never be trivial. Dialogue can be very uncomfortable and people will be unwilling to stick with it if the subject matter seems to be unimportant or irrelevant to *them.*
2. *Manage context not content.* Provide an empty canvas. Enable people to 'suspend disbelief' and to hear each other out. Let go of massaging the outcomes.

3. *Keep things public.* Everyone stays in the room in order to hear as much as possible of what others have to say. Records should be kept and should not be edited; asides should be audible to all.
4. *Let the difference be seen and heard.* Keep the complexity. Let people tell their own stories. Don't facilitate the differences away.
5. *Manage the language.* Encourage people to state the purpose of what they say, outlaw jargon, ensure everyone understands the implications of what is being said.

The partnering grid is a powerful dialogue tool because it reveals much of what might otherwise have remained hidden or implicit. By showing partners where all perceptions of the partnership lie on the grid, misunderstandings become apparent and explanations for puzzling behaviour present themselves.

We have had many helpful suggestions for different labels on the partnering grid, but we have found that the ones we use and the spatial relationships between them, although not ideal by any means, give people a 'script' and a place to start. They beg the right kind of questions; questions that reveal the tensions and contrasts that generate agendas for conversations that matter.

Language at work

While communication receives much attention, language itself is treated uncritically as if it were simply a window to reality.

The common sense view of language is that we use it to describe the world we live in; that our reality is concrete, indisputable, and open to a method of description that does not distort what actually exists, be that physical, social, emotional or political. Indeed we do use language to describe what we see, experience and understand about the world.

To focus only on this aspect, however, is to ignore its most powerful function. Language also constitutes the reality we experience. Our offers, rejections, invitations and denials position those to whom we speak in ways which have a direct influence on what it is they can do.

The power in language is in its performative function: in what it enables us to do together. This is mediated utterance by utterance, response by response, in a complex interplay of identity, ambition, relationship and power.[6]

Put simply, the effect is quite different if we invite others to share in the plans we are making to when we slam a contract on the table and demand a signature. Surprising though it may seem, we have worked with partners who have begun with the latter and been puzzled by the fact that their partners were not rushing to share their hard-won knowledge with them. Or even the reverse, where partners began with broad democratic intentions, only to produce a contract from a bottom drawer when the going got rocky.

The real challenge of partnering communication is to recognize that business partners change. A relationship which began in *hearts and minds* may not stay there for long, just as a partnership which gets into *gridlock* may not be stuck there forever.

Not only that, the common tendency to skim over the surface of conversations which threaten to address anything remotely connected to the 'soft' aspects of trust (and mistrust), honesty (and deceit) or ambition (and power), often means that our assumptions about our partners are based more on our own projections than on anything they may have actually said.

So what does all this mean in practice?

Most importantly, it means that partners need to be more sharply aware of the language they use and the effect it has in terms of what does or does not get done as a result of it. Often our patterns of business talk work in ways which actually undermine our good intentions. Breaking such habits is an imperative for *radically new* partnerships.

Here are some of the tools we have used to help partners do just that. They may give you some ideas of your own.

Some tried and tested techniques for making 'common' sense

A casual observer of many business meetings would be forgiven for concluding that common sense is the least common of the senses. Here we describe how partners can help themselves and each other to turn their conversations into productive ways of producing 'sense' that they have in common. Or, to put it another way, of making 'common' sense. The techniques described here deal with making space, making meaning and making decisions.

Making space

But doesn't that mean . . .

(*. . . I can get a word in, at last?*) We spend at least as much time listening to ourselves in meetings as we do listening to what others have to contribute. As MIT professor Bill Isaacs said, during one of his dialogue training programmes: 'In meetings we have two modes of being: speaking and waiting to speak.'

Grabbing a turn keeps most people's attention focused on what it is they want to say and on spotting the next appropriate opening. The distribution of available turns is usually controlled by the person who holds the notional chair and, most likely, the last word. Meanwhile, most of the time, most people are engaged in nudging the conversation one way or another to get the space they need to take it more their way. The conversation is often much more about whose turn it is, than it is about what the group as a whole needs to do with the issue at hand.

This can be transformed with the use of a few Lego bricks.

With the bricks as tools, and the simple guideline of every time someone takes a turn they also take a brick, the dynamics are subtly but dramatically transformed. People can collaborate, if they choose, to share turns more evenly. It is immediately visible to all who is hogging the floor space and who has said nothing or, more importantly, who is controlling the conversational output and whose views are simply not part of the picture. After all, buy-in is not a psychological activity, it is a conversational one.

I absolutely agree, and let me add . . .

(*. . . something completely different.*) We all have a wide range of elegant mechanisms for changing the subject and getting away with it. In fact, many of us are so skilled at this that meeting agendas are often lip service to a reality where the first theme is addressed formally followed by round after round of point scoring and theme snatching until five minutes before the end when the last six agenda items are rushed through. We are accustomed to meeting dynamics which emphasize personal ground over shared understanding.

One common characteristic of the traditional work encounter is a phenomenon which seems to be based on the assumption that you will be able to say more of what you want if other people in the room are disabled from making their points. This dynamic does a great deal to undermine a partnership's ability to explore alternatives from a variety of perspectives.

What is being traded in this instance is not turns, but themes. It is possible to break down conversations into two main blocks: new topics and themes, on the one hand, and everything which is said to support or disagree with those themes, on the other. Who gets to introduce new ideas and whose contributions are passed over are built in the interplay between the themes people hold and the space they can find to bring them into the group.

By using Lego bricks, counters, sugar lumps (or whatever is to hand) to externalize the thematic dynamics, individuals become more able to give away more space for others to make their points, while at the same time observing that to do so actually gives them more space to introduce new themes themselves (see Box 6.1). This forces groups to be more explicitly aware of the moves each person makes and its impact on what the group as a whole is able to do as a result.

Box 6.1   *Making space for different views*

Each group member begins with two bricks, which are to be placed one at a time into the centre whenever a speaker introduces what he or she regards to be a new theme. Having no bricks left to play disables a member from introducing anything new until another member chooses to give a theme brick away. The payback from the act of giving a brick away is to take two bricks from the centre in return.

The bricks make a pragmatic, not an ethical point. There is nothing wrong with getting one's view heard or making sure that the conversation goes one way rather than another. We are not suggesting that we must never use language to achieve our own purposes. The question is whether or not these ingrained meeting mechanics serve those purposes when we seek a radically new collaboration.

Making meaning

The imperative in the context of complex partnerships is the ability to create enough shared meaning to co-ordinate successful completion of a task. A complex brainstorm (see Box 6.2) can help partners to see their similarities and differences and still do things together.

Box 6.2   *The complex brainstorm*

After the initial pooling of ideas, a round of questions begins where the aim is to find out more about what matters to others in the group and why. Informed by the answers, interest groups or individuals then circle the most important items as they see them in relation to the group as a whole and not, as is customary, to build up their individual case. By circling the items and links in different colours, the group can together read the connections between their issues and the way each member of the group sees them.

At a governors' meeting at an infant school, convened to review the past year and plan the coming year, it was felt that the usual practice of splitting the governors into sub-groups to look at four areas – finance, staffing, curriculum and community communication – provided no opportunity for any of the governors to see the 'whole picture'. New conversational rules were introduced to manage this new attempt to find holistic understanding and solutions.

Participants found the atmosphere created by the rules rather strange, so there was much testing of assumptions and guarding of responses, but the sub-groups duly produced their diagrams for the whole group. Those of the finance and staffing groups were virtually identical, but the maps of the curriculum and community groups were totally different, both from each other and from the finance and staffing diagrams.

The differences were thrown into sharp relief when two mixed groups were asked to plan an event five years hence, designed to celebrate the school's achievements. They had to consider who should be involved and how the occasion should look and feel. Some passing references were made to staffing problems, but neither group mentioned finance once and the celebrations were remarkably similar, consisting largely of the wonderful things the children were learning and the very healthy state of community relations.

It seemed that although community and curriculum were pretty remote from the current reality, they were widely seen as the school's life blood. Curriculum and community could no longer be regarded as incidental to planning. They had to be at the centre of the process because, if they were not, the governors could not help bring about the future they all wanted for the children.

Given time, people with different languages or different ways of seeing the world, come up with their own mechanisms to check meaning that guarantee action occurs. This meaning tends to be built over time through the experience of both understanding and misunderstanding in relation to the action resulting from what is said. But time, unfortunately, is the one thing most partnerships cannot afford.

Building a shared context for action requires that partners explore the multiplicity of their perspectives rather than argue about which is more real. The data partners need to make sense of is as much in the relationships between them as it is in the nature of their environment.

Furthermore, as we saw in Chapter 3, that environment is very different depending on where each stands. Such interrelated complexity falls out of view in most meetings. Even a 'brainstorm' after an initial wave of participation is subject to the purposes, interests and resource control of the most influential party. What usually gets named agreement is really no more than a fraction of the picture available. It is on that fraction, nonetheless, that action flags tend to be planted – no surprise then that the extensive flipchart lists of actions carried away from brainstorming sessions rarely get done.

In a complex brainstorm, however, the relational complexity is part of the picture. This enables a group to understand a wider range of meaning from the start and to explore a much broader range of possible actions as a result. Rather than leaving the critical synthesis to the influence of the facilitator, a few guidelines enable the group to manage collective sense making for themselves. By making both commonality and difference visible, the meaning of consensus shifts from shallow compromise to common understanding.

Making decisions

Data without decision will not bring results. In spite of this, many working groups employ conversational mechanisms which ensure maximum politics for minimum output. The nature of the game is often based on keeping agendas hidden and personal purposes veiled.

The lack of a single control centre in most partnerships, however, means that without a process for revealing a little more of the purpose of particular moves, people can have no reference point with which to work out where individual actions connect with the whole. As a result people often play at decisions to keep up appearances but never actually do anything about any of them.

Partnerships sometimes need help in breaking their own decision dead-lock. Traditionally hidden knowledge about support, conflicts of interest, and personal purposes need to be more public. People can then co-operate about what it is they can do together, rather than compete about who is going to do what to whom. Such working dialogue can condense several months of politicking into a two-hour conversation which shelves the scoring of individual points and puts the construction of collaborative action in its place (see Box 6.3).

Box 6.3 *The decision circle*

Individuals write two or three critical actions they want to see or make happen on separate pieces of card. Sitting in a circle, each person in turn reads out what is on their card and places it in the centre of the circle. If individuals feel that the action proposed can happen now, then they leave it in the centre. If, however, anyone feels for whatever reason that it is not doable, then they take the card from the centre and place it outside the circle. During this part of the conversation, the only talking allowed is the reading of cards: all other com-ments need to be stored up for later negotiation. When it comes to discussing the cards, and to negotiating their final destination, people can then say what-ever they wish in whatever way they wish. Rather than use language as swords and shields, however, they reveal what they are trying to achieve with what they are saying in addition to the actual comment they wish to make.

For example, the conversation may begin with a participant wishing to challenge the removal of a particular card. There are many possible motivations for such a challenge, ranging from a suspicion that the card has been removed in order to block a particular line of conversation or action, to a wish to know whether the card could be made acceptable by a change of wording.

The requirement to make purpose explicit obliges speakers to think carefully about what they trying to achieve (in terms of the actions proposed and the conversation), before saying anything.

Someone might say for example: 'The purpose of this is to find out why you removed my card. Was it because you don't want to see my suggestion

Box 6.3   *The decision circle (continued)*

happen?' To which the answer may be: 'The purpose of this is to assure you that I support the idea, but would like us to look at the words. I took it out because the way it is worded makes me think we're taking too much on.'

Or someone might say: 'The purpose of this is to check whether you support the basic idea, as I imagine you do. Why did you take the card out?' To which an answer might be: 'The purpose of this is to tell you that you've got that wrong. I took the card out because I don't think the idea will work.'

The system gives people a structured way of checking out each other's assumptions and purposes and so enables decisions to be reached that everyone supports.

Wiring for conversation

Technology provides a framework in which people can get the results they need. It drives some of the working practices and communication channels needed to get work done. Yet often technology, although an accepted part of the ways things will be, is seen as adding yet more data to the confusion of getting results in an interdependent world. People are snowed under with data and demands: more e-mails, more voice mail, more meetings, more projects, more cuts and more pressure. It seems impossible amid this mass of information and imperative to concentrate on the right priorities.

As membership of groups who make core decision widens, managers are often left disabled by the lack of meaningful data with a broad enough perspective in an interdependent system. In one organization we worked with, more than 50 individuals needed to be present to take any decisions that required the commitment of resources.

Partnerships are equally constricted in their decision-making capacity. While multi-perspective groups can access more of the data they need, they either fail to reach agreement or are found wanting in the reach of their mandate.

It is not the people who are at fault here, but the inability of current information and communication solutions to give meaningful measures of success in the moving picture of an interconnected environment. Without mechanisms to make sense of the complexity of interdependence, people are not sure what to measure and how to keep it alive in the partnership. Consequently, most have little or no way of knowing if they are getting the results they need and cannot, no matter how committed they are, make the networked reality deliver.

Try as we may, we will not discover a way to re-engineer people. The current rate at which individuals are bombarded with data flows from the assumption that they have the capacity to make sense of it all in order to inform their decisions. Yet this information, in itself, is worthless. The value comes not in the information but in how people are able to interact with it to give it meaning. The moving picture of the networked economy is unlikely to freeze frame long enough for any one individual to make sense of it; and without meaning there can be no action.

Individuals do, of course, make sense of data, but they are not, and have never been, able to make sense of all of them alone. In spite of this, the widely held conviction that the locus of all meaningful action is within the individual has led to the development of a whole generation of computing applications which are aimed at enhancing individual capability. There is little that individuals can achieve, however, if they are prevented from holding meaningful conversations with others. Yet, remarkably, the main thrust of technological development still sits within the wiring carried out for information transmission and not for conversation.

In *radically new* partnerships, the power to decide lies not in the hands of those currently with the resources, but in the mechanisms for collective sense making. An organization is not a scientific configuration of autonomous decision-making units with computer-like abilities to process numerical information and communicate verbal outputs. It is an intricate web of dynamic relationships in which people negotiate meaning they can use in a moving feast of promises, invitations, commitments and opportunities.

The imperative for the future of partnership communications is to balance the need for individual data with a generation of computing applications which reinforce the need to build shared meaning in conversation with others.

In both face-to-face meetings and in asynchronous, online conversations from different time zones around the globe, partners need ways of having sensible conversations about:

- the changing context within which people are operating
- the collective resources available for the task

- interpreting performance and results
- taking decisions
- how the work gets done in relationship with others.

The partnering grid makes a start by providing a map for conversations where many perspectives are accepted as real, but there is still some way to go.

Getting there

A partnership has to develop a common working language to help partners understand each other and their circumstances because, without such public, collective understanding, it cannot maximize the extent and scope of its common ground or exploit to the full its opportunities.

Such common languages need two distinctive characteristics – the habits and rules of working dialogue and an integrated communications system that reflects, rather than refracts, natural human interaction. The media are in a sense the language. They provide its rich variety and the careful choice of media can ensure its efficiency and effectiveness.

Dialogue is not only valuable in face-to-face communication. Its distinctive rules should ally to the whole communications system and are often easier to apply in other media. For example, rules of dialogue are embedded in the editorial policy for the letters page of the *JLP Gazette*, the house journal of the employee-owned retailer, the John Lewis Partnership. Any partner can write a letter to the editor, anonymously. Insofar as space allows, all letters are published and, if the letter is a request for information, or a complaint, as many are, the manager concerned has to respond to it.

Similar rules can be embedded in new media, such as e-fora and permanent conferences, where people are given space to vent their frustrations, point fingers and generally give voice to their fears or sense of injustice.

Sometimes these rules of openness are treated as a licence to be personally abusive, to launch subversive attacks on the organization's strategy or the conduct of its managers. It is often tempting, in these circumstances, to break the rules by applying censorship, but that would merely reinforce older conventions that prevent dialogue.

Information technology can, in fact, be a powerful catalyst in the creation of a *radically new* partnership, because the process of designing an appropriate IT network requires a discussion of interaction and decision making that can reveal previously hidden rules and conventions.

By making rules visible, technology makes them changeable, not because the IT system itself is equipped with X-ray eyes, but because people are made aware of the weakness of the rules during the design process. As Lancaster University's Honorary Professor of Knowledge Technology Bob Lewis puts it, 'technology forces the folklore under the microscope'.[7]

Strict turn taking, for example, can seem an unnatural constraint on the individual freedom so prized in western culture. Some will rebel against the rules and 'dialogue tyrants' will have to enforce them, because there is always a strong temptation to return to more traditional styles of interaction.

The important point is that discomfort during dialogue is quite natural. The new space to which the rules of dialogue can take partnerships or other working communities is more creative *because* it makes people more anxious. You must support people and help them deal with their anxiety, but the anxiety, particularly your own, must never be designed out.

Our emphasis in this chapter on working dialogue should not be taken to mean that we believe dialogue rules should govern all business conversations. The challenge is to choose the most appropriate medium for the environment and objectives.

If the context points to the left of the grid, where power is centralized and fixed, the traditional conventions of communication are appropriate. In the middle of the grid, where power remains centralized but knowledge is distributed and there is more participation, the kind of space provided by quality circles, for example, is needed.

When the context is on the right of the grid, where power and knowledge are both widely distributed, conventional styles of conversation do not work because they prevent the expression of multiple views and the revelation of the complex collective purposes that inspire collaborative action. It is here where new, rule-governed 'space' is needed for conversation and it is the leader's job (see Chapter 7) to know when it is necessary and to make it available.

Ultimately, relationships between individuals will determine whether or not a partnership works. There is little that leaders can do to force people to get on with and trust each other, but they can create the right climate and foster virtuous habits, such as the habit of dialogue.

Story from the front ...

Dialogue of the deaf

The Mondragon federation of industrial co-operatives, in the Basque country in northern Spain, is often held up as a model of how industry should be organized. It is indeed an outstanding example of an alternative organizational form and one where the spirit of common ownership and co-operation reconciles conflicting interest and promotes industrial harmony.

Inspired in the post-civil war period by the vision and hard work of a young Roman Catholic priest, Jose Maria Arrizmendiarrieta, the Mondragon Co-operative Corporation now comprises 150 companies, a workforce of 60,000 and a turnover of 8 billion euros in 2001.

There are few more remarkable success stories of partnership and co-operative entrepreneurship. Without the initial push born of a *hearts and minds* approach, no one doubts than none of this would have happened.

But 'co-operativistas' in Mondragon are under no illusion that working from a shared set of values on a strategic level always leads to harmony in operations. In fact, the stories told there of change and renewal usually centre on a difficult and often prolonged period of negotiation and challenge. Mondragon is, above all, a story of partnership through time. Rather than take a snapshot of a business relationship to pronounce it sick or healthy, in Mondragon worker–members at all levels have stuck with bigger *hearts and minds* pictures at the same time as recognizing both the inevitability and potential for creativity in *gridlock*.

To understand one such conflict that broke out at one of the federation's member companies in 1989, it is first necessary to understand the 'constitutional context': the distinctive system of corporate governance that prevails throughout the Mondragon federation.

To reflect their employee ownership, it is stipulated in the constitutions of all the members of the Mondragon Co-operative Corporation that everyone has an equal vote in the 'Asamblea General' (general assembly – equivalent to the annual general meeting of shareholders).

The co-operative is governed, on a day-to-day basis, by three councils: a 'Consejo Social' (social council), a consultative body that meets regularly and gives information and guidance to the 'Consejo Rector' (governing council, equivalent to the non-executive tier of a two-tier board of directors) and the 'Consejo de Direccion' (managing council, equivalent to the executive tier of a two-tier board or the executive committee of a unitary board).

The members of the social and governing councils are elected by the general assembly and members of the managing council are appointed by the governing council.

To many western corporate governance experts, the system will doubtless appear unwieldy and not conducive to responsive or decisive management, but it has worked well over many years at Mondragon and the potential for conflict between its constitutional components remained latent until an abrupt change occurred in the company's economic context towards the end of the 1980s.

Like most conventionally owned European manufacturers at that time, the company came under serious pressure from recession and intensifying competition and, by 1989, it was in imminent danger of collapse.

The governing council responded to this crisis in an entirely conventional way, by appointing a new chief executive (CEO) with a brief to do whatever was needed to return the troubled company to profitability.

His prescriptions were conventional too; he hired consultants and embarked on a rationalization programme that included substantial reductions in shop-floor and management staff, a de-layering of the hierarchy from six to three levels and an attempt to induce everyone, not the just marketing people, to be more customer focused.

The CEO was a strong and decisive leader. He had a clear idea of what had to be done and he implemented the rescue plan in a firm, if somewhat brusque, way. Within three years, the firm was not only back from the brink but doing well again. It had all the hallmarks of a successful turnaround.

But the CEO's refusal to reflect the more onerous workload – the inevitable consequence of the downsizing and de-layering in higher pay, created a feeling of unease among the worker–members and sowed the seeds of what would later become bitter disputes between the social and governing councils.

In terms of the 'partnering grid', the CEO's rescue operation shifted the relationship between managers and worker–members from the original *hearts and minds* to the *arm's length* box and many worker–members did not like it. Although the company was doing well again, it had lost its social cohesion and the worker–members split into two camps: those who saw the CEO as a hero and those who felt his decisive action had destroyed the precious spirit of co-operation that many who work within the Mondragon federation find so inspiring.

The social fragmentation was mirrored by disputes between the social and governing councils, both of which, as noted earlier, are elected by the general assembly. But although the debates between the two councils were vitally important, not only for the firm but also for the Mondragon federation as a whole, no real dialogue ensued. The social council kept criticizing the parlous state of labour relations, while the governing council contented itself with declarations of support for the CEO and the management. Positions became deeply entrenched and the relationship became increasingly polarized.

The smouldering conflict ignited in 1993 when, in response to renewed competitive pressures, the CEO proposed an adjustment to the 'remuneration ratio'; the maximum multiple the highest salary can be of the lowest. Such ratios are vital symbols in producer co-operatives and 'alternative' management firms the world over and people are always very sensitive about them.

Ben & Jerry's Homemade, a successful American ice-cream maker founded by Vietnam veterans Ben Cohen and Jerry Greenfield, is famous not only for such confections as Wavy Gravy, Chunky Monkey and Cherry Garcia, but also for holding annual general meetings in fields, giving 7.5 % of profits to charity, buying ingredients from disadvantaged people and generally promoting the values and ethos of the responsible corporate citizen.

From the start of the firm in 1977 Ben & Jerry's distinctive personality was also reflected in a rule limiting the highest salary to five times the lowest. In 1991, the reality of the market for senior executives obliged the firm to increase the ratio to 7:1 and, in 1994, as Ben & Jerry's began looking for a new CEO to replace Ben Cohen, it removed all constraints on what it could pay its top managers.

In the Mondragon company's case, the maximum pay laid down in the company's constitution was 4.5 times the lowest wage. The CEO proposed, for exactly the same reasons that led Cohen and Greenfield to modify and then abandon their maximum, that the multiple be increased to 6.5:1, to reflect the extra pressure on managers in the more competitive climate.

Heated debates instantly erupted in the social council about the role of the CEO, what happens at other kinds of company, what it means to be a co-operative and how much voice in such matters the worker–members should have.

The managers insisted they had to have more discretion in the salary area and that if their proposals were not approved, the company could go under in the highly competitive climate. The social council would have none of it and called for a general assembly.

The CEO spoke at the assembly and said that the system could not work if his hands were tied. He argued that if everyone had to participate in everything, managers could not manage, claimed the firm's constitution was a democracy of delegates not of direct representatives and warned that how well people were paid depended ultimately on how well the firm performed.

This was like a red rag to a bull for the social council and, as one observer put it, 'a very strong, verbal confrontation' ensued.

The CEO reflected on his style and adopted a softer line. He began coaching a successor with whom he shared the leadership and he tried to 'educate' members, by sending them on courses to learn why the changes were necessary. He even put managers through a programme to improve their co-operative skills.

As the arguments about the pay ratio and the role of the CEO rumbled on, the company continued to do well and before long the outside world recognized the CEO as an able leader. Early in 1996 he was promoted to the MCC (the governing Mondragon Co-operative Corporation) and was named 'businessman of the year' by a local employers' association.

The successor he had been grooming took over and proved to be more disposed to dialogue. Relationships appeared to improve for a time, until, in an attempt to get the company closer to its customers, he proposed holidays should be staggered from June to October and no one should take more than two weeks in August.

It may seem trivial, but as pay ratios are to co-operators, so August holidays are to Spaniards. Spain is shut in August. It was an incendiary proposal and the worker–members rejected it out of hand.

The new CEO tried to win them over to his point of view, with presentations and training programmes and urged them to think in more business-like ways, but although there were some good open discussions and an acceptance of the need for dialogue, neither side would budge on the holiday issue.

Positions became entrenched again. Each side lost confidence in the other and the mutual lack of trust made it impossible to promote the positive aspects of the relationship.

Everyone had a voice and everyone had their say, but although all knew they had to break the deadlock and understand the other side's position, the talk went round in circles. As one participant put it, it was a 'dialogue of the deaf'.

The odd thing was that, although the individuals on each side of the argument changed, the battle lines remained in exactly the same position and the language never altered. The company became unglued. Dialogue between managers and worker–members ceased and the partnership, which began in *hearts and minds*, and which the previous CEO had tried to move to *arm's length*, ceased to exist.

Fortunately, the new CEO had a good feel for the tensions between business and community needs and began to organize a different kind of conversation. Multi-stakeholder teams were convened, which began to discuss less controversial business issues in less confrontational ways and, as common ground was revealed, people slowly began to emerge from their entrenched positions.

In 1997, some people took holidays either side of August and when others refused to budge, temporary worker–members were appointed under special constitutional arrangements to keep the firm going during the traditional holiday shut-down.

The new CEO has had some disagreements with his managers over the composition of the new project groups, but the company is still doing well and as members continue to work together on business tasks, the wounds inflicted during the confrontation healed over allowing worker–members to focus on getting the work done.

References

1. *The Man of Destiny*, G. Bernard Shaw (play manuscript, 1897).
2. Redefining the European Re-structuring Agenda. A Study of Re-structuring Performance and Future Re-structuring Challenges, in *Redefining Restructuring: Toward Solid Growth* (A. T. Kearney, 1997).
3. *Discovering Common Ground*, M.R. Weisbord (Berrett-Koehler, 1992).
4. *The Learning Company. A Strategy for Sustainable Development*, Mike Pedlar, John Burgoyne and Tom Boydell (McGraw-Hill, 1991).
5. *Perspectives on Dialogue*, Nancy Dixon (Center for Creative Leadership, 1996).
6. *Language and Power*, Norman Fairclough (Longman, 1989).
7. *Ownership and membership of a virtual team: the perspective of a research* manager, Bob Lewis (paper presented at IMD, Lausanne, September 1996).

7

Someone at the helm

Divide and rule! Fine saying;
Unite and lead! Safer refuge
Johann Wolfgang von Goethe, Spreche in Reimen

No aspect of management has attracted more attention in recent years than the changing role of the leader. Leadership has become the primary focus of management debate, and leaders are its undisputed stars. It is therefore ironic and rather alarming to find that, while hundreds of books have been appearing about what leaders should be doing in the brave new 'globalized', e-enriched business world, the status of business leaders in industrialized societies has been declining steadily.

Business leaders were not held in high esteem in the early 1990s when a Lou Harris poll[1] found that barely 40% of American office workers believed the statement 'management is honest, upright and ethical' was 'very true'. In the European Union, the figure was only 26% and in Japan, a mere 16% of office workers thought management was 'honest, upright and ethical'.

Since then things have got even worse. One of the most important, and least commented on, consequences of the Enron and WorldCom debacles in 2002 was a further sharp decline in the standing of business leaders within society at large and thus a further erosion of the vital social consensus on which the liberal capitalist system is based.

A *Business Week*/Ipsos Reid survey published in June 2002 (see Table 7.1) asked people: 'How much confidence do you have in those running big business?' The answer was alarming. The headline is that, in December 1999, just 13% of American adults had little or no confidence in those 'running big business', but two and a half years later that figure was up to an alarming 30%.

Table 7.1 *Public confidence in those running big business*

% of all adults	A great deal	Only some	Hardly any	None at all
December, 1999	15	69	13	n/a
Summer, 2000	19	58	17	n/a
February, 2002	14	54	25	5
June, 2002	16	52	25	5

Source: Business Week, 24 June 2002

Some explanations for the decline in the status of and faith in leaders are obvious, but the trend began before the Enron and WorldCom affairs and the urgent debate about corporate governance they inspired. Misguided leaders and dubious accounting practices clearly contributed to the most recent crisis of confidence, but business leaders have been losing their lustre for other reasons. Some say 'globalization' is exposing their parochialism and their inability to grasp the implications of planetary management and claim the modern global business organization has outgrown the ability of one person or team to lead it.

Another variation on the theme is that the increase in the rate of change and technological convergence has caused the required leadership reaction time to become so fast that traditional leaders no longer have enough time to gather and process the relevant information.

Others suggest the decline in the stature of leaders is a consequence of an increase in the intensity with which their performance is scrutinized; that it is not so much that business leaders are becoming less competent, as the extent to which they are being held responsible for the performance and the conduct of their firms is increasing.

James Meindl says it is our 'romantic' idea of leadership that causes us to attribute great potency to leaders – to praise them extravagantly when they succeed and to damn them when they fail. We believe it is time to recognize that the age of romanticism is over and we must face up to the real causes of organizational success and failure.[2]

It is not just employees and investors who pass judgment on the leaders of organizations. A host of environmental, social and pressure groups, claiming to speak for an ever growing constituency of stakeholders and good causes, are pointing fingers at individual leaders and holding them accountable for all the ills of the world, ranging from global warming and the reduction in bio-diversity, to inner-city deprivation and rising unemployment.

A parallel theme in the new leadership debate is the idea that the role of leaders and leadership is changing: that new circumstances demand a new paradigm of leadership. The old idea of the leader as a general who plans, deploys and issues orders should be replaced, it is suggested, by new roles such as 'orchestrator', 'conductor', 'co-ordinator', 'ambassador', 'mentor' and 'coach'. If leaders can no longer do what they used to do, the argument goes, they must find a new role for themselves that addresses new needs.

Some say the complexity of the modern environment makes the old-style, hero model of leadership inappropriate, because one person cannot grasp all the implications of all the variables. The future therefore belongs, according to this view, to leadership teams or 'systems'. Some acknowledge that the leadership 'pair' has long been 'standard' in publishing (editor/publisher) and film making (director/producer) and this principle of divided leadership offers a way forward for other industries and organizations.

The debate about whether CEOs should chair boards of directors and the view in Europe, and increasingly now in the USA, that they should not, is leading to the emergence of a 'separation of powers' principle in business, similar to the constitutional separation of 'legislative' from 'executive' power in a democracy: the leadership pair of a non-executive chairman and a chief executive in the business world.

The paradox of leadership in an age of empowerment is confronted head on in partnerships. Which, if any, of the traditional functions of leadership are still essential in enterprises consisting of 'empowered' organizations and individuals? If strategy emerges from the exploration of common ground, what service do leaders supply?

Leadership and the grid

Leaders often over-estimate their power. Sometimes they fail because they lack the ability to 'envision' and implement effectively, but their failure is often a failure to understand the 'context' created by their environment and objectives. They want things to be 'controllable' and behave as if, with their power, they can make them controllable.

If a change programme fails, it is often because someone, somewhere has not done his or her homework on how others perceive the context. You can try to command and control directly, or dominate indirectly through 'culture', but ignoring other voices does not make them go away or erase the thoughts that inspired them. Leaders must understand the context if they are not to waste time, money and commitment on programmes that have no chance of success.

The leadership variant of the partnering grid (see Figure 7.1) can help to fit leadership style to partnership context.

The language of the grid makes it easy and, we believe, very appropriate to think of leadership as having different roles in each of the six boxes.

On the left-hand side of the grid, the leadership, whether an individual, a pair or a group, dominates in *command and control* and integrates in *hearts and minds*. As we have seen, these two boxes are appropriate when knowledge and power are concentrated. In both cases, leaders can and do abrogate to themselves the right to manage both the ends and the means; they set the partnership's direction and control implementation either directly, through the power invested in them, or indirectly, through the cultures they design and impose.

In the *command and control* and *hearts and minds* boxes, where difference is dysfunctional and must be minimized, leaders are involved in everything, from 'envisioning' and selling plans and strategies, to controlling all the

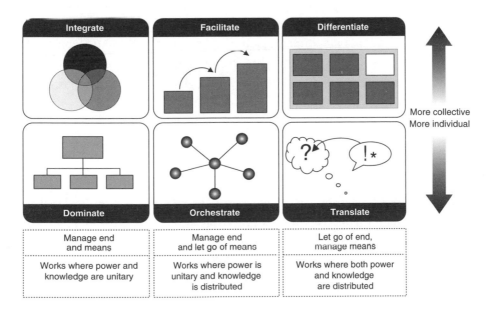

Figure 7.1 *Leadership grid*

minutiae of content and processes. They need no containment system, because everything is already under their own control.

Individuals feel secure, but imprisoned.

In the middle of the grid, power is still concentrated in the hands of a leadership oligarchy, but knowledge becomes more widely distributed and it becomes impossible to dominate or to integrate. In *arm's length*, where difference is tolerated but ambition is modest, the characteristic activity of leaders is 'orchestration'. In *do and review*, where ambition is greater, the emphasis is on facilitation. In both cases, the lack of a central brain or control system obliges leaders to relinquish their power to control the means and to content themselves with controlling the ends.

The distinction between 'orchestration' and 'facilitation' reflects subtle but important differences in how a wider distribution of knowledge is seen. In *arm's length*, it is seen as a regrettable fact of life that requires a less hands-on approach to management. In *do and review*, contrariwise, the wider distribution of knowledge is seen as a competitive challenge that can only be met effectively if people are free to gather new knowledge and act on it, within the constraints of the overall strategy.

In *arm's length* and *do and review*, where difference is tolerated a different kind containment makes an appearance. Because difference has to be 'lived with', leaders have to relinquish some of their control of content, but they retain control over process. They become the keepers of methodologies and although they do more facilitating than their counterparts on the left side of the grid, they still orchestrate and direct. Outcomes are not planned in great detail, but leaders control them indirectly through their power over processes.

Individuals feel less secure, but more liberated.

Leadership style will come under pressure to move even further to the right of the grid when both power and knowledge are widely distributed because, in partnerships of this kind, attempts by individual partners to facilitate or orchestrate will put the survival of the partnership in jeopardy. The characteristic activity of a leader in *gridlock* is translation; leaders feel obliged to spend a lot of time interpreting and trying to understand to ensure agreement before the partnership acts. In *radically new*, partners are more sanguine about their differences and the communications problems associated with them. They not only believe difference is the engine of the partnership; they revel in and celebrate it and the only understanding they feel a need for is the understanding that they need to act together.

On the right of the grid, where power and knowledge are widely distributed, a new role emerges for leaders which we think of as 'managing the process of collective sense making'.

In the *radically new* box, where difference is seen as the engine of the enterprise, leaders relinquish control over content *and* process. This makes people feel free, but insecure and anxious. Some containment is still needed, therefore, to keep anxiety within bounds and legitimize difference, but it is a softer and more flexible containment than that provided in the middle of the grid by the leadership's control over processes.

It takes the form of a set of general 'behavioural' (as opposed to specific 'process') rules such as: scientists invent and publish; artists create and exhibit; accountants analyse and report, and rules of dialogue, designed to reveal common ground and permit the precious, shared resource of difference to be fully exploited.

The containment also includes rule 'policing' (through signals, rather than instructions), which encourages the trial and error learning characteristic of neural networks. People are left to their own devices and are only made aware of the rules when they seem to be about to break them. Security comes not from instruction, but from knowing everything that is not proscribed is legitimate.

The presence of such a minimal, but good enough, containment, leads to high levels of creativity and the gradual emergence of mutual trust and a shared sense of destiny.

We will spend the rest of this chapter exploring some of the main implications of this conception of leadership, beginning with some practical examples of leadership effectiveness in a context on the threshold of *radically new*: the scientific research team.

Leadership in a knowledge-based world

Academic research is a great laboratory for students of leadership, because it is done by teams of gifted, highly motivated individuals dealing in pure knowledge and, more particularly, in the business of breakthrough innovation. It is a microcosm (perhaps the prototype) of the knowledge-based businesses that many management experts expect to be the dominant business life form over the next decade – businesses focused on growth through innovation, as opposed to cost containment through process efficiency.

In an un-published doctoral thesis, Rose Trevelyan examined the leadership styles at various academic scientific research groups.

One of the groups was led by George, who had an outstanding track record in his discipline, but had stopped doing his own research ten years earlier. He saw his role as securing funding for the team and acting as a control node for communications within the team and between the team and its external environment. Team members spoke to each other through him but the team as a whole was not very communicative and, when they did talk, they usually argued.

George reacted to events and his team lacked any rhythm of work, apart from the rhythm provided by the funding cycle.

Another group was led by Alice. She was also a scientist of high repute but, unlike George, Alice was still very involved in her own research. She spent a lot of the time working at her 'bench' alongside her colleagues, who both admired and respected her. She was not a 'charismatic' leader, but her team recognized her talents, valued her experience and heeded her advice.

She had no particular view of her own role in the team, but when asked, her colleagues would say that she was a source of knowledge about 'the business of science' – about how to 'do' science and how to succeed as a scientist – and had 'great contacts'. Team members were highly motivated and satisfied with their working environment. The atmosphere was friendly and stimulating and there was a great deal of talk about practically everything.

Alice gave her team a work 'rhythm' by instituting a series of meetings at which one team member gave a presentation which was then discussed. This was good practice for team members because presenting ideas and research results to peers is one of the main ways ambitious scientists achieve success. Alice organized the presentation schedule but did not lead the discussions – in the context of these discussions she was just another member of the team.

These meetings, and the collaborations they inspired, helped the individual scientists by providing different perspectives on their work and exposing their assumptions to challenges from peers. Their different backgrounds (from many different areas of chemical engineering) were made available to all and the meetings became places to explore differences that often proved useful in each other's research. Constant communication and a habit of collaboration (helping each other with experiments, techniques and interpretations) also helped to make good use of the differences within the team.

Members of Alice's team said they felt 'there is someone at the helm'. They did not mean by this that there was a captain on the bridge, who had a clear idea of where the ship was going. They meant there was someone who could be relied on to get funding, point out the shoals and rocks that lay ahead, warn people in time for them to take evasive action and generally encourage the research directions most likely to be successful.

There is no overall direction in academic research. You have to 'conjecture boldly' and follow where your ideas and experiments lead. A unitary sense of direction is actually quite dangerous in science, because it constrains the imagination and leads researchers to ignore the oddities or inconsistencies that often lead to the acquisition of new knowledge.

But although a narrow direction can be counter-productive, there is a lot to be said for establishing a clear framework for research and having someone around who is familiar with all the rules and conventions that must be followed if 'good' science is to be recognized as such by the scientific establishment. Young scientists need role models and mentors to 'show them the ropes' and to help them get connected to the right networks. They need to be able to talk to people who are 'streetwise' in the business of science – who know the best journals to be published in and the criteria editors use when selecting papers, what conferences and seminars to go to, who to speak to or consult with and what prizes to enter for.

Research scientists do not need someone to tell them what to do or where to go in their research, but they do need counsellors and mentors to help them when they get stuck and tell them when they are barking up the wrong tree, veering off track or failing to publish enough or cultivate enough contacts and connections.

In short, they need people who know the 'rules of the game' and are always available, because they are always there. Alice's team had all that and it showed in their results.

The best measure of a scientific research group's performance is publishing success, measured by an index of the number of articles published, weighted by the 'visibility' (visibility is the best available proxy for quality) of the journals. The Institute of Scientific Information publishes a Science Citation Index, which ranks journals according to how often they are cited and awards them an 'impact factor' that measures references in all journals in subsequent years to the articles in the journal in any one year.

Trevelyan used an index based on the number of articles the groups published in each journal, multiplied by the journal's impact factor, to measure the performance of each research group. The score for George's group was 2.7, the average for all the groups was 4.2 and the score for Alice's group was 4.9.

She also used a measure of job satisfaction – from Hackman and Old-ham's Job Diagnostic Survey – as an outcome variable. The average for researchers in George's group was 5.2, the average for all groups was 5.3 and the average for Alice's group was 6.0, out of a maximum of 7.

Scientific research teams provide a useful analogy for the kind of context in which leaders of modern, knowledge-based companies operate – contexts designed to produce breakthrough innovation to drive growth.

We need to go beyond this, however, because in contexts where *radically new* is the only appropriate operating model, power cannot be embodied in an individual like a team leader. Our model of leadership must accommo-date situations in which all rules and rulers can be challenged and where nobody is 100% in control.

The new leadership

Trevelyan's work on research teams helps to define the styles of leadership needed within knowledge-based, innovation-led organizations. Combining her insights with those produced by the grid and by our partnering research, we can draw up the following provisional list of new guidelines for leadership:

- Use signals, not directions and focus more on *who* people are than on *where* they are or should be going.
- Accept, reveal, validate and celebrate difference, by seeking it out and making it part of the common ground.
- Take nothing for granted. Challenge all assumptions, question motives (including your own) and bring the inevitable struggles for power and influence out into the open.
- Be there or be spare. By being there you can help to legitimize both individual and group action.
- Let go. Trust people, because only the trusted become trustworthy.
- Recognize that groups can only get energy and direction from the energy and ambitions of their members. Leaders must, therefore, follow as much

as much lead and spot on behalf of the whole group where the energies of the group are pointing and what that means for common action. Leaders must continue to do their own work, to maintain their own expertise, rather than relinquishing all work content in favour of exclusively directing others.

This list of guidelines is provisional because it begs more questions than it answers. It advocates a renunciation of the traditional leadership roles without providing specifications for a new role.

Reading between the lines of the guidelines, however, reveals the shadow of a shape that encompasses, but does not control; that supports, but does not direct; and that proscribes, but does not prescribe; that is expert in its own right; that above all seeks *connections*. It is a negative kind of leadership, like J. D. Salinger's *Catcher in the Rye*, which stops those led from falling off cliffs, but is otherwise content to facilitate and create a container in which tasks can take place.

Another way to put it is to say that in *radically new* partnerships and most loosely linked enterprises, the role of leadership is to build and maintain a 'soft container', within which the led are able to pursue their own purpose and plans and thereby help to generate the group's 'emergent' strategy. No easy task, of course, and it is made doubly difficult by the requirement in *radically new* that this 'soft container' must be constructed and maintained collectively, not by an individual or group.

Leading by containing

In *radically new*, leadership creates spaces many for different kinds of interaction and is extremely sensitive to the nuances of context. Nowadays there are more voices and more competing realities than ever before and in partnerships where power and knowledge are both widely distributed, and are constantly being traded, there is no escaping them.

Some kind of common sense must be made of all the cacophony and this cannot be done by the traditional idea of leadership as embodied in an individual because the partnering 'context' does not permit it.

Context is other people and cannot be understood unless everyone involved has a chance to express his or her views and reveal his or her aims, assumptions and prejudices. Context as 'other people' maps the common ground and acts as the frame of collective action.

The frame of action the leadership must divine and maintain consists not of the mechanical cause and effect levers that managers are taught to identify and manipulate, but of a general ambience within which creative, collective action is encouraged. In W.P. Kinsella's story, *Shoeless Joe* (on which the film *Field of Dreams* was based) the hero is told, 'If you build it they will come.' That is the leadership's job: to build it and act as the attractor that draws them in.

As we have seen, the leaders of today's organizations must realize that in modern environments they cannot realize static long-term plans. They can, however, guide their enterprises, teams and organizations into a creative space, by tuning their various elements, such as the level of anxiety (too little is as bad as too much), the distribution of power and knowledge, the level, frequency and transparency of communications and the metrics that form the language of those communications.

In *radically new*, power is very widely distributed but a vestige of leadership remains, in the form of a collective, self-managing system that contains activity, while allowing people to challenge and subvert it.

Many questions are begged here about what constitutes 'good enough, but not too good' containment and control systems that provide 'a little bit more than not enough' security, but the concept of 'leadership' as some kind of disembodied *container* is a useful starting point which allows us to expand our provisional list of leadership guidelines.

Systems that say 'no'

An axiom in the philosophy of science is that, although it is impossible to 'verify' a theory, it *is* possible to 'falsify' a theory. Scientific advance is driven not by the verification of new theories, but by the falsification of old theories, and the way to strengthen or 'corroborate' a theory is to think of experiments that could disprove it.

It is the same with *radically new* leadership. The way to help people is not to tell them what to do, but to create a system that will 'warn' them when they are barking up the wrong tree, re-inventing the wheel or heading down roads others have proved to be dead ends.

With this 'guardian' role comes a responsibility to handle the consequences of advising people when to stop, through building the rapport and connection that allows you to explain why it is advisable to stop, to describe the likely outcomes of not stopping and to do all this without discouraging people from exploring new avenues and continuing to take risks.

The able, self-confident professionals on whom most enterprises rely do not like to be told they are wasting their time. They much prefer to be patted on the back, from time to time, and left to get on with it. The stop signal must be used sparingly and, when using it, the user's credentials for doing so must not only be in plain view, they must also be debatable.

People will not heed advice to 'stop' or change course unless they believe those giving the advice are 'qualified' (usually through deep expertise) and they will not learn from being stopped unless they can challenge the advice and negotiate the timing and terms of any future use of the stop signal. Most important of all, they are unlikely to heed a leadership system that will not heed them when they tell *it* to stop.

Being the rules

The credentials of leaders to issue 'stop' signals consist not so much of their wisdom and power of patronage, as their intimacy with the 'rules', the breadth and richness of their networks and experience and above all their *alignment* – both their internal congruence and their connectedness to those around them.

Alice was qualified to say stop because she was seen as streetwise in the ways of science. Her canniness and intimacy with the 'goings on' within the scientific establishment were seen by her colleagues as an invaluable team resource – a sensing system which extended their own knowledge of right and wrong and good and bad.

A goal-seeking group operates within a set of rules. There are social rules governing behaviour within groups, rules of etiquette governing interaction between groups, and meta-rules associated with occupations and professions that govern the behaviour of individuals and how they conduct themselves in relationships. The rules of interaction are implicit but fixed on the left of the grid, mutable in the middle, and explicit on the right. Few are law like, in the sense that they can be clearly articulated; most take the form of conventions governing social interaction and are thus context specific.

The rules are embedded in good leadership systems, but are not written down and posted on noticeboards. They are part of the context and invoked only when necessary.

Rules channel and focus rather than constrain and it is the job of leaders and leadership systems to know them, show how they all fit together, apply them, explain them and *be* them.

Managing paradox

However well endowed with rules and however well led, individuals and teams are always encountering inconsistency, conflict, ambiguity and paradox.

For example, there is ever present tension between the interests of the individual, or individual partnering organization, and of the collective. Where the commercial interests of the individual firm are at odds either with the interests of others in the partnership or that of the partnership as a whole, uncertainty, conflict and ambiguity build. We yearn for security in an increasingly unstable world and our desire for certainty grows as uncertainty crowds in on all sides.

All this ambiguity and conflict create anxiety. Anxiety is invigorating in small doses, but there is a limit to how much people can handle. Containing anxiety is a vital leadership role in working communities poised on the creative brink of total instability, not by removing it, but by confronting it and coming to terms with it.

Effective leaders can show people the constructive aspects of conflict. They can say it is OK to be different, that 'paradox is where the action is' and that it is quite possible for two apparently conflicting views to be equally true. They can translate, interpret, summarize and show how apparently conflicting interests are reconciled on common ground. They can give people a sense of their place and of the group's place in the confused uncertainty and answer the big questions such as 'what's the point?'. And, above all, they can pay attention to the health of the relationships that will enable the group to make sense of the uncertainty, to move forward together and to have the bandwidth to detect the 'weak signals' that indicate the way forward.[3]

Internal strife, damaged relationships and lack of rapport all take up valuable focus and attention, creating an internal 'white noise' that may prove deafening to the vital signals from the outside world that will give the partnership hints of which way to turn.

One partnership suffering a major breakdown of trust managed to turn down the 'white noise' sufficiently to recognize the primary cause of conflict between the partners. Competitive activity between the partnering organizations in another area of business, outside the boundaries of the partnership – two wholesale distribution divisions – was causing strife within the partnership itself. Such was the importance of maintaining the relationship in the partnership – and the business value it brought – that one of the partnering organizations committed to disposing of its wholesaling division.

Rewards and feedback

The vast majority of organizations that form partnerships do so with enthusiasm and high expectations. They start off, in other words, highly motivated. A good leadership system ensures the initial fiat of enthusiasm is sustained.

Academic research exemplifies this challenge, because scientists are highly motivated individuals who see research projects as stepping stones. They want to be members of successful research teams because the team's success will enhance their own reputations and take them a step nearer to achieving their own goals, such as winning a Nobel prize or leading their own teams.

What they want of a leader, and what could deter them from leaving to join another research team, are guidance and feedback on their progress towards their personal goals and personal recognition. They must be paid enough to contain their material anxiety, of course, but they also want credit, where credit is due – they want their ideas and contributions to group success to be fully and publicly acknowledged by inclusion of their names on published papers, for example, or mentions in public presentations of group research.

The leader's role is vital, because these attributions and acknowledgements are usually in his or her gift.

The desire for recognition – the *right kind* of recognition – is very strong and people must be confident that it will be given, when appropriate. They must trust their leader to know what kind of recognition is appropriate, to distribute it fairly or to explain the reasons for withholding it. Faith in just rewards is part of the containment leaders and leadership systems must provide and it is as necessary in a partnership as in an academic research team, because without it relationships will be strained and may come apart.

But reward systems in partnerships are complex and must function effectively for both individual member organizations and the partnership as a whole, even if that means overruling incentive systems within individual member firms that subvert the good of the whole. Reward systems help to define cultures and, in partnerships, what individual members see as a 'just reward' may vary enormously. It is vital, therefore, that everyone should know what each of their partners wants and that their wants will inevitably change over time. It is the job of the leader, or leadership system, to ensure everyone gets as much of what they want as possible and that reward and measurement systems are fluid enough to keep up with changing needs.

Recognizing transitions

The social dynamics of a collective enterprise change as stages of projects or projects themselves are completed and as people join, develop and move on. When new recruits join, they need a lot of guidance and support, but as their confidence grows, they become more self-sufficient and more familiar with the 'rules of the game'.

In a partnership, of course, the most important 'rule' is that the rules of the game are complex patchworks of different sets of rules and members need to know to whom each rule set belongs, whose interest it serves, how it can be questioned and who may do the questioning.

Leaders must be aware of these subtle transitions and act accordingly. They must know when erstwhile apprentices have become masters and sometimes they may need to hand over leadership to others who have become better qualified or have a better sense of the key issues in a particular area or project.

It has been said that one of the most important jobs of a leader is to make him- or herself redundant. The leadership of a flock of flying geese shifts from one bird to another when the wind veers, the flock's navigation system demands a course correction or the leader simply tires. In enterprises like partnerships, where power is widely distributed, the baton of leadership must be free to move.

Transitions from patron or protector roles to colleague or follower roles (and back again), show the leadership system is working well; that people are growing; that pride, jealousy and the battles for power and 'face' are not distorting or petrifying the group's containment.

When leadership is seen as fluid, rather than embodied in a person, leaders ask themselves if they are the right people to lead at this particular time or, given the skills and experience of team members, whether there is a need for any conventional leadership at all.

Leadership experts often claim that, although a talented group of musicians can make wonderful music without a score, an orchestra cannot operate without a conductor. The orchestra has been billed, by the doyen of management writers Peter Drucker among others, as a model for business organizations, and orchestra conductors, the real stars of the classical music world, are seen as role models for business leaders.

Harvey Seifter,[4] executive director of the Orpheus Chamber Orchestra, explains how this unique musical institution became the world's leading chamber orchestra – *without a conductor*. A democratic system, known as the 'Orpheus process', takes the decisions made by the conductor in a conventional orchestra.

The process is not easy or very efficient, in terms of time, but it is very effective. The Orpheus has won four Grammy awards and the quality of its concert performances allows it to charge higher fees than any other chamber orchestra in the world.

In his foreword to Seifter's book, Richard Hackman, Professor of Social and Organizational Psychology at Harvard University, says: 'Rather than relying on a charismatic, visionary leader…might it be possible for all members to share responsibility for leadership and for differences and disagreements to be sources of creativity rather than something that should be suppressed in the interest of uniformity and social harmony?'

If a competitive advantage can emerge from democratically shared leadership in the classical music business, there is no reason to suppose it could not emerge from a similar process in a conventional business. It would not work in all businesses, but it has a lot going for it in 'knowledge-based' partnerships where the overwhelming priority is attracting and keeping good people. CEOs of such companies will read the Orpheus labour turnover rate and weep. The average tenure of the orchestra's musicians is 20 years!

Keeping it going

When strategy is emergent and granular – in the sense that it consists of a series of more or less discrete projects – the question arises: 'How do you persuade employees to turn up after the last project has been completed and the next has yet to begin?' What, in other words, maintains the enterprise's integrity and energy when plans are shifting and emergent?

There will always be discontinuities in relationships; times when you pause for breath and reflect on whether you have gone as far as you can with this group towards achieving your goals and it might be time to move on. If the group is to survive, people have to be persuaded the best is yet to come. This is best done, not by passionate appeals for unity, tirades against traitors or by the painting of grand visions, but by establishing, through dialogue, whether the group's common ground has been fully explored or whether more opportunities exist to prove the group is still worth more than the sum of its parts.

Relationships should be abandoned when they have ceased to create value, but many partnerships are ended prematurely because members have not taken the trouble to explore the full extent of the 'common ground' – it has just become too hard to make it work. We believe that, for most partnerships, it is best to assume that common ground grows as it is acted on and that abandonment is almost always a mistake.

But no partnership should be entered into without an exit strategy in place and a clear view of what would trigger that exit. In fact, the fluidity of a partnership structure is its great strength and source of value – appropriately timed exit merely creates an opportunity elsewhere; as Tom Stoppard put it, 'Look on every exit being an entrance somewhere else'.[5]

The key to staying or going is dialogue – constant, ongoing, open dialogue. But if no one insists dialogue occurs at regular intervals, no one can know whether remaining or abandonment would be a mistake until it is too late.

Making communication public

Successful partnerships are obsessive communicators. Members talk a lot with one another, are deeply interested in what is going on outside the group in areas of interest to them and their colleagues and are always interacting and learning in their efforts to improve their understanding.

You do not have to encourage people to learn. They learn spontaneously and often unconsciously. It is part of leadership's task to ensure this natural human hunger for knowledge is always kept well fed and that their knowledge is rendered useful by sharing. Leadership systems cannot direct learning, because they cannot always know what is important, but they can help create spaces where the habits of learning and open communication flourish.

Of course, learning in partnerships is less straightforward than in single organizations. Quite apart from the basic issues of intellectual property and fear of loss of competitive advantage through sharing knowledge, in partnerships learning takes place through multiple organizational layers, multiple cultural filters and back and forth across organizational boundaries – more like a neural network than any more hierarchical, bounded structure.

Neural networks learn automatically through a technique known as the 'back propagation of errors'. When attempting to solve problems, they guess, test the guess against reality, record the imperfections and then send them back through the network to tune the strength of connections between neurons.

Like a neural network, for learning to occur spontaneously in a partnership, you need a set of interesting problems and enough information to test the accuracy of each successive guess at the solution. Leaders can help to achieve this by making information available transparently across organizational boundaries; encouraging open, non-recriminatory discussions of errors; and doing all they can to increase the connectivity between the nodes of the partnership network.

Leaders should be gate openers as well as gatekeepers. They can facilitate communications and the flow of information by providing appropriate 'means' (databases, meetings, access to experts etc.) and by taking charge of the group's (as opposed to the individual's) social interaction.

Rose Trevelyan observes that when left to their own devices, scientists can be so preoccupied with their work that they switch off socially and become incommunicado. The intense focus is necessary, but it should be interrupted occasionally by meetings and socializing.

This advice holds true for members of a partnership starting to drift apart. They would do well to take note of Trevelyan's observation: 'Scientists have to be encouraged to be a group because their basic attitude is that they are on their own.' For scientists, read business partners.

From leaders to leadership systems

Leadership in a distributed organization is not a matter of commanding, controlling or motivating, but of providing suitable containment in the form of rules, conventions and support systems. The containment is soft, in the sense that it can be pushed into new shapes by those contained, but strong in the sense that it is in no one's interest to breach it.

The leadership system can play its own part in self-management, but cannot control it. Its role is to provide space where people feel secure (but not too secure) and to equip it with the tools, sensors and support partners need to understand each other and to decide what to do together.

Stories from the front

Leading for Value

Partnering is a strategic theme of increasing importance in the global chemical and pharmaceutical industries. In their different ways, Eli Lilly and Dow Corning demonstrate the value of partnering leadership, and the ways leadership flexes in different partnering contexts.

Eli Lilly has over 300 alliances, for example with biotech firm Centocor. Centocor has developed a drug called ReoPro, which helps prevent cardiac complications from devices inserted in clogged blood vessels. Lilly led ReoPro through the U.S. FDA approval process while Centocor was being acquired by Johnson & Johnson, demonstrating how leadership can pass between partners to accommodate changing circumstances.

Lilly works hard at developing and strengthening its relationships. To help ensure strategic aims remain aligned, it tries to understand the partners culture, and the business pressures under which it operates. To help ensure the partner's commitment to the alliance, it tries to minimize its internal staff re-shuffles, and appoints a senior sponsor for each alliance. To help ensure fairness, each alliance has its own alliance manager, who acts as an ombudsman, and sides with the partner as often as with Lilly. In this way the leader's task and allegiance flows freely across the boundaries of the relationship.

Dow Corning began serving coatings industry customers in the 1940s, developing the first silicon-based binders for high-heat maintenance coating applications like industrial smokestacks. In the decades since, Dow Corning has developed a long list of innovative products, including multi-functional silicone additives for paints, inks, coatings and adhesives; water repellents for the most demanding substrates and environments; and unique binder technology for solvent-borne, water-borne, solventless and powder coating systems. Through partnership in service and technology, Dow Corning has earned a global industry reputation for silicon-based solutions.

Dow Corning's leaders are of note for the sheer longevity and persistence of their relationship. Although more than half of all partnerships fail, Dow Corning's has lasted for generations. In 1942, top management from Dow Chemical Co. and its customer, Corning Glass Works, met to discuss joint development of silicon resins needed for the U.S. war effort. The result was Dow Corning. What began as a handshake agreement and an initial investment of \$5,000 from each side continues trading to this day. The partnership has proved resilient to even the toughest challenges, including a recent Chapter 11 bankruptcy filing inspired by a spate of product liability lawsuits, strongly contested by Dow Corning.

Building on this legacy of partnership, Dow has built strategic alliances with numerous other companies, including BASF and Samsung Electronics who have agreed to develop and refine inter-layer dielectric applications using Dow Corning technology.

In another illustration of handing the leadership 'baton' back and forth across organizational boundaries, Dow has partnered with technology companies including Sun and Documentum, to deliver the technology advantage they seek.

When Dow Corning decided to work with Sun five years ago, it cemented a partnering relationship for developing advanced technological solutions. Dow Corning actively participates in the evaluation of new technology solutions from Sun and is consistently an early adopter of these technologies. 'We have moved with just about all the technology shifts that Sun has introduced both in terms of servers and storage. Sun's technology curve has stayed ahead of our needs' said Ken Karls of Dow Corning's Global IT Engineering and Support Group.[6] Equally, Sun was Dow Corning's technology supplier of choice because they too committed to working in partnership with other vendors. 'Two technology suppliers were unreceptive to a mixed vendor environment. Sun, on the other hand, demonstrated its commitment to a truly open architecture even where it meant interfacing with a different vendor's systems'.

References

1. Quoted in *Credibility: How Leaders Gain it and Lose it, Why People Demand it*, J. Kouzes and B. Posner (Jossey-Bass, 1993).
2. *The Romance of Leadership*, J. Meindl, S. Ehrlich and J. Dukerich, *Administrative Science Quarterly*, Volume 30, 1985.
3. *Alpha Leadership: Tools for Business Leaders Who Want More from Life*, A. Deering, R. Dilts and J. Russell (Wiley, 2002).
4. *Leadership Ensemble*, H. Seifter, (Times Books, 2002).
5. *Rosencrantz and Guildenstern are Dead*, T. Stoppard (Faber & Faber, 1967)
6. Quoted at www.sun.com

8

On trust and conflict

And trust me not at all, or all in all
Alfred, Lord Tennyson, *The Idylls of the King*

In this final chapter we will see what light the partnering grid can shed on the role of trust in all enterprises, not just partnerships, and discuss the very different perspective it offers on the problem of conflict.

It has been popular over recent years to attempt to design and manage organizational culture. If, the logic goes, we can design a workspace where people's commitments are based more on trust and respect than obligation and control, then we will be able to create a more responsive and flexible workforce.

This has led to a widespread belief that intangibles such as trust, identity, commitment and knowledge are manageable inputs to a different 'culture'. If we look at partnerships from this perspective, it seems that conflict is a result of getting the design wrong.

We maintain that organizational culture or 'the way things get done around here' is influenced more by the way people talk to each other on a daily basis than it is by designs on paper. Plans, policies, strategies and visions do not speak to each other, people do.

Commitment, confidence and trust are outputs, not inputs. They are built on ongoing relationships that accommodate changes in conditions, objectives and personnel. Organizations from this perspective do not 'have' cultures, they *are* cultures.

Francis Fukuyama says the social virtues and the 'art of association' vary from culture to culture and that high-trust cultures, such as Germany's and Japan's, are better than low-trust societies, such as France's and China's, at creating large organizations which do not rely for their integrity on family ties and state ownership.[1]

In recent years, management writers have also identified trust as a crucial ingredient in building and maintaining large organizations.[2,3]

If, as all these writers claim, trust (or 'social capital' as Fukuyama also calls it) is the 'glue' that binds associations of people together without the help of kinship ties or state ownership, no book about partnering would be complete without a discussion of its sources and significance.

Most recent work on partnering has assigned a central role to trust and the avoidance of conflict. We do not. In our model of partnering, trust is not a pre-condition or *sine qua non*, but merely a consequence of acting together in a 'context'. And as contexts vary, so the quality of trust that develops within them varies.

Dimensions of trust

It is important to distinguish between varieties of trust, because Fukuyama would have us believe that there is only one kind of trust and only those fortunate enough to have grown up in 'high-trust' societies will be capable of forming durable partnerships with each other.

In the new age of global markets, this cultural limitation on partnering is unacceptable and also inappropriate. Trust is not, or at any rate not only, a simple homogeneous quality or potential that exists in some cultures, but not in others. We must, instead, look at trust as something that emerges from collective action and takes various forms.

The partnering grid provides such a perspective.

Figure 8.1 shows that the degree of trust rises as a partnership becomes more ambitious and the kind of trust needed to sustain ambitious partnerships changes as one moves across the grid.

The variety of trust that can move partnerships from *command and control* to *hearts and minds* is a trust born of similarity and consensus. People trust each other here because they regard each other as similar and bound by the same rules. The way to promote this kind of trust and move up the grid is to choose similar partners and develop a strong, shared culture.

The trust that can move partnerships from *arm's length* to *do and review* is a trust that comes from experience and the growth of mutual respect. People learn to trust each other by working well together and, as each project is

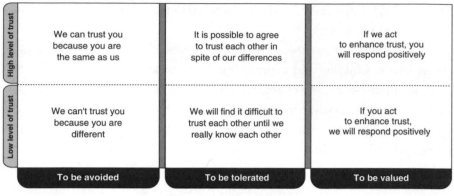

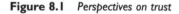

Figure 8.1 *Perspectives on trust*

successfully completed, trust grows. The way to build this kind of trust is to foster two beliefs: that the relationship will last and each project, in addition to being value creating in its own right, is an opportunity for the partners to learn how to work better together.

The trust that moves partnerships from *gridlock* to *radically new* is a trust born of recognition of mutual interests. People trust each other because they see no reason not to. They are aware of the risks, but have concluded there is too much to be gained by both or all the partners for it to be in any partner's interests to defect from the partnership by cheating. The way to promote this kind of trust is for partners to be honest with each other about their strengths, weaknesses, dreams and worries, comfortable with the differences between them and so visibly committed to the relationship that it is inconceivable that any partner would place their individual interests above those of the partnership.

In other words, trust is related to perceived risk. It exists in *hearts and minds* because risk is low; it grows in *do and review* as risk reduces and it is endemic in *radically new* because the perceived risks are overwhelmed by the expected mutual rewards.

Talking about risk, and how it rises and falls and changes form as you move around the grid, can often be illuminating.

In one case three partners answered a set of questions about trust and the results were used to plot their positions on the partnering grid. They were all in the right-hand column, but two were close together at the top while the other was less than half-way up.

It turned out that the reason for the difference was that the third partner (caught in *gridlock*) saw a type of risk in the partnership that did not apply to the other two and had not occurred to them. All three partners were intrigued by the revelation and it was discussed at some length.

Following the discussion, the isolated partner said: 'Now that you understand how I see my particular risks, I'm less worried about them.' The diagnosis itself and the discussion that followed brought about an upward movement to a more trusting relationship.

Trust acts as a form of control – an individual 'self-control' that emerges unbidden from joint action leading to mutually rewarding outcomes.

The case against partnering

The case against partnering is that, although the idea of bringing together two or more complementary sets of skills or resources without anyone paying for them is attractive in theory, it takes no account of the incompatible cultural baggage also brought together in such unions.

The sceptics will accept that the technical and process linking required in partnering can be accomplished relatively easily and harmoniously, as long as the links are installed at the right level, and they may even admit that skills can also be orchestrated without too much difficulty, as long as the right people are doing the orchestrating.

'But that's the easy part,' they will argue. 'The real problem is that this linking of processes and skills will only create the promised value if individuals from quite different cultures can learn to work well together, if not on day one, at least within a few months.

'Speed is of the essence nowadays and companies can't afford the months and years it may take to bed down partnerships, still less spare the management resources needed to resolve the rows that will always break out when no one is entirely in control.

'Those who advocate partnering should try it. It's very difficult to manage two contrasting cultures. They are always rubbing each other up the wrong way and, without the authority that comes with ownership, the conflict soon gets out of hand and destroys any chance of capturing the synergy.

'It's the same as when an American spacecraft docks with a Russian one. The docking mechanism works OK in that the two craft become physically one, but once the crews have embraced, that's it. The crews can't do any useful work together, because they can't understand what the other crew is saying. And even if they were all bilingual, cultural difference would prevent all but the most trivial collaboration.'

It is true that the personal conflict on which many partnerships founder is mostly caused by a rubbing together of the cultural baggage that comes with the technical, process and skills contributions of the partners. But there is no getting away from it. Whether one likes it or not, this is the nature of partnership. Skills, however technically compatible, cannot be 'docked' to create the joint capability the partners seek, without an effective docking of the partners' respective cultures.

There is nothing wrong with the analysis of the sceptics. The mistakes they make are in the conclusions they draw from it.

The first mistake is their implicit assumption that the problem of cultural conflict is peculiar to partnerships and that, when they acquire a company, they absorb its culture. This is obviously wrong. Cultural tribalism can be just as virulent between predator and prey as it can between partners and, because money has been paid, it can be much more costly.

The second, more serious, mistake is to assume that conflict is a barrier to effective 'docking' and that the only associations between companies that create value are those in which all is sweetness and light, within a peace imposed by *force majeure*.

Aspects of conflict

The conventional view is that conflict is undesirable, because it distracts attention away from management's proper external concerns, wastes resources on resolving conflict and can put the integrity of the whole enterprise, be it company or partnership, at risk.

Richard Pascale challenged this view and argued that conflict is a creative force that endows organizations that tolerate and even foster it with more creativity and flexibility than their consensus-seeking rivals.[4]

There is too much evidence to support both views for it to be reasonable to reject either. Conflict clearly does foster creativity and flexibility and, equally clearly, it can become pathological and lead to the termination of working relationships.

The trouble with the obvious resolution to this dilemma, that partnering firms should foster enough conflict to generate creativity but not so much that stability is jeopardized, is that it is hard to judge, beforehand, the point at which conflict stops being a virtue and becomes a vice. When those persuaded by Pascale's thesis begin to vie with each other, to see who can crank up conflict levers furthest, they have no way of knowing how far they can go before it is too late.

We do not see such contradictions and dilemmas as begging to be permanently reconciled. Quite the reverse in fact. We see the struggle to make sense of (and *do* something about) seemingly contradictory positions as the source of change and innovation.

The partnering grid boxes themselves can be seen as relationship spaces where people have found a temporary resolution to conflicting ideas.

Command and control steers between speed and accuracy; *hearts and minds* between control and creativity. *Arm's length* gives respite from the tension between deficiency and identity; *do and review* between efficiency and adaptability. *Gridlock* is a way of dealing with the contradictions inherent in situations that demand stability but present uncertainty, just as *radically new* needs to deal with both complexity and unpredictability while delivering innovation.

Our partnering work has convinced us that the common sense view of conflict is based on a false premise. Conflict is not, as many assume, an independent, unmanageable variable of co-operation that occurs spontaneously whenever cultures meet. It is, rather, a symptom of attempts to minimize difference.

No conflict between American and Russian astronauts is likely after a space docking, if no attempt has to be made to bridge the cultural abyss between them. But when a joint work programme is to be undertaken, cultures as well as spacecraft have to dock and the chances are the process would generate conflict, if not between the crews themselves, at least between the mission control teams planning the work.

When one begins to see conflict as a 'docking' procedure, as a language or set of protocols for fitting significantly different partners together, the question 'what is the right dose of conflict?' is replaced by the question 'how different can two prospective partners be and still achieve a mutually satisfactory docking?'

The power of difference

Although there is no generally accepted body of partnering 'lore', there is no shortage of opinion about partnering. There are passionate evangelists and passionate sceptics; there are those who see it as strategic and those who see it as little more than a label with which to embellish outsourcing arrangements and acrimonious negotiations with suppliers. There are those who advocate intimacy and those who urge arm's length relationships; those who believe in sharing everything with their partners and those who jealously protect what they see as their 'core competences', on the grounds that within every partner there lurks a potential competitor.

Our view is that, although disagreements about what a partnership is (or should be) and what it might become profoundly influence how those involved in the partnership behave, many are misconceptions and others are not really disagreements at all but become, when looked at from a different angle, equally logical and perfectly compatible ways of looking at the same relationship.

Furthermore, our research shows that difference, whether or not it leads to conflict, is a necessary ingredient in ambitious partnerships because without it, there can be no synergy and no positive sum to the partnering game.

Conflict is often simply a testing procedure: a way to compare, explore and understand the merits of different ideas, approaches, attitudes and values. Too many partnerships are abandoned because the behaviour they inspire is seen as 'conflict' (destructive and to be avoided), when the same behaviour could just as plausibly have been seen as argument, debate or dialogue, and thus constructive, and to be welcomed.

One of the virtues of partnerships is that, if differences are not so great that the union collapses, the partners can learn as much about themselves as they do about each other. People who have their own ideas, attitudes and values, but respect yours, are people you can do business with.

Difference is the source of creativity. Conflict is a sign of growing intimacy; a sign that partners have seen through their apparent similarities and begun to enter new partnering territory. Whether perceived as conflict or debate, docking or alignment behaviour is part of the mutual exploration of cultures and attitudes. It can get out of hand, of course, but as long as partners are compatible and have a positive sum game to play together, it need not.

In an ambitious partnership, a lack of conflict is a bad sign because it suggests a lack of the mutual exploration that makes partnerships creative.

But not all partnerships have high ambitions and the degree of conflict it is worth enduring depends, ultimately, on the context – the environment and the objectives of the partners. There are as many reasons for partnering as there are partnerships and it would be pointless to struggle with difference if all you wanted to do with a partner was to prepare the ground for a divestment or to present a united front to a regulator or a potential competitor.

The trouble is that, until now, the literature on partnering has offered no guidance on what partnership qualities are suited to particular partnership objectives. Partners may be clear about their objectives, but unsure about what kind of relationship they need and how much conflict they will have to encourage or tolerate to achieve them.

It is too hit and miss. Before partnering can become a reliable solution to the wide range of business problems to which it is theoretically applicable, it must cease to be a black art and a lottery and become, if not a science, at least an art of a whiter hue that people can talk about sensibly and, by talking about, learn to understand.

As T.S. Eliot concluded:[5]

We shall not cease from exploration
And the end of our exploring
Will be to arrive where we started
And know the place for the first time.

References

1. *Trust: The Social Virtues and the Creation of Prosperity*, F. Fukuyama (Free Press, 1995).
2. *The Trust Factor*, J. O. Whitney (McGraw-Hill, 1993).
3. *Stewardship*, Peter Block (Berrett-Koehler, 1993).
4. *Managing on the Edge. How Successful Companies use Conflict to Stay Ahead*, R. Pascale (Simon & Schuster, 1990).
5. Little Gidding, *Four Quartets*, T.S. Eliot (Faber & Faber, 1944).

Afterword

The dos and don'ts of effective business partnerships

Every business partnership is different, taking place in a particular set of circumstances and with its own special business outcomes and relationships to manage. Each faces specific challenges and offers unique opportunities. It is impossible to set out prescriptions for partnering that will be true for all partners, in all circumstances. However, we do think there are some generic dos and don'ts that are worth bearing in mind as you pursue partnering excellence.

We offer you the following checklist in the spirit of sharing lessons learned from past successes – and failures. If you have other ideas and suggestions for this list, we would love to hear from you.

1. **Do** remember that marginalization, not conflict, is what prevents partnerships from succeeding. Stay in touch with your partner, stay in dialogue – even if the conversations are painful and difficult.
2. **Don't** assume conflict is a sign of impending failure – or that its absence is a guarantee of success. Conflict surfaces issues – make sure you pay attention and resolve them rather than smoothing things over.
3. **Do** make sure you have facts available to avoid getting pulled into arguments about perceptions and accusations of shifting goalposts. Be rigorous in defining value for all partners up front – and track them religiously throughout the life of the partnership. Make sure all parties are involved in the tracking and that the performance dashboards are visible and accessible to all.

4. **Don't** rely on facts alone – expectations, perceptions and assumptions are the stuff of partnerships and are as important to success or failure. Take the time to bring these ambiguous elements into the partnering dialogue – and be open to what they tell you.

5. **Do** recognize that there are many different approaches to partnership that will work in some contexts – and not in others. Notice your environment, the fit between your objectives and the style all parties bring to the partnership. Use the assessment tools presented in this book to guide your thinking. Take action to address misalignment.

6. **Don't** worry if harmony is most noted by its absence. Most partnerships generate some and, more often, a lot of conflict. Threatening and defensive behaviour is common. Focus on the value all parties expected to achieve from the relationship and take action to maximize it. Use task to improve relationship – not relationship to improve task. It is by working together to achieve a common goal that relationships improve. Focusing on the relationship per se may make it worse not better.

7. **Do** remember that culture is extremely unlikely to shift to accommodate stretching goals; objectives will decline in ambition to fit the prevailing culture.

8. **Don't** forget it is your response to difference, rather than difference itself, that is the underlying cause of conflict. Notice that difference can be a powerful source of creativity and transformation and find ways to harness its potential.

Appendix A
To acquire or not to acquire – that is the question...

Acquisition can be an effective and value-adding strategy – in some circumstances. In others, partnering could prove more capable of adding long-term value to your organization. The trick is identifying which strategy to pursue for maximum effect.

All partnerships and acquisitions have unique strategies, players, resources and value potential. Of course, the decision will be made based on the specific value drivers and competitive context of each individual case. However, we believe there are some signposts, some indications, of where partnering rather than acquisition might be worth exploring.

Use the following checklist as a prompt in your strategic deliberations. If you have more yeses than nos, partnering may prove to be a more effective option than acquisition.

	Yes	No
Unpredictable growth in your industry	❏	❏
Turbulent or unfamiliar environment	❏	❏
Widening stakeholder community	❏	❏
Accelerating rate of change	❏	❏
Strong constraining external forces	❏	❏
Intense political instability	❏	❏
Multiple pressure groups	❏	❏
Conflicting objectives or purposes	❏	❏
Power widely distributed	❏	❏

Complex, discontinuous change	❑	❑
Knowledge held widely across the whole system	❑	❑
Value widely spread across whole system	❑	❑
Multiple objectives or purposes	❑	❑
Broad and influential stakeholder community	❑	❑
Competitive advantage to be gained through breakthrough, discontinuous innovation	❑	❑
Diverse cultures, complementary skills and approaches	❑	❑
Need to keep resources fluid for future strategic moves	❑	❑
Uncertain future – unclear on long-run value from other company	❑	❑
Open culture – able to build on difference and create value	❑	❑
Track record of creating sustained value in alliance with other organizations	❑	❑
Uncertain 'acquisition currency' – questions around ability to finance an acquisition	❑	❑

Appendix B
Partnering grid self-assessment

To give readers a feel for what it is like to work with our partnering grid, we invite you to complete the following questionnaire.

It is derived from a diagnostic tool we developed based on our research findings. The tool is based on priorities, preferences and relative weightings and is designed to enable partners to compare and discuss the different ways their partnership appears to them, to unravel tacit assumptions and so build a richer picture for effective collaboration.

The calculations required for the full diagnostic do not lend themselves to pen and paper, so we have used a much simpler approach here which, although not statistically valid, captures the feel of a conversational diagnosis. For a full and statistically valid mapping of a large group of partners, the partnering grid software is the most appropriate tool, but we believe that this diagnosis should give you some interesting 'food for talk'.

Each of the six sets of statements that follow relates to one of the boxes on the grid. Scoring the statements and adding up your total score for each of the sets will give you a picture of the relative weightings you currently place on the six approaches to partnering.

It is unlikely that a person, or organization, will display a preference for only one style of partnering. The diagnostic points to a current dominant preference, not to an absolute position. Moreover, a box which presents itself as dominant when considering one task may be virtually non-existent in the context of another task. We change our grid positions in response to actions and even within a conversation. It is important, therefore, to have a particular current task in mind when answering the questions and not to focus in a general way on the relationship itself.

Bald results mean little without some idea of what they mean for the individual concerned. For this reason, we suggest you get at least one other person to fill in the questionnaire focusing on the same partnering task, so that meaning can be extracted from the differences that emerge.

Think of a critical work or business task in your partnership and tick the box that best represents how you currently view this task.

To complete your questionnaire, tick the most appropriate box and then score each statement as follows:

Strongly disagree	Disagree	Neutral	Agree	Strongly agree
1	2	3	4	5

Questionnaire

	Strongly disagree	Disagree	Neutral	Agree	Strongly agree
1 Our organizational cultures are strongly aligned	❏	❏	❏	❏	❏
2 We enter the partnership with a strong shared vision	❏	❏	❏	❏	❏
3 We meet regularly to address emerging needs	❏	❏	❏	❏	❏
4 We emphasize clear communications	❏	❏	❏	❏	❏
5 Knowledge is widely distributed across the partnership	❏	❏	❏	❏	❏
6 The more we plan things, the better	❏	❏	❏	❏	❏
7 We develop new ways of working at the interface	❏	❏	❏	❏	❏
8 We are concerned about conflicting objectives	❏	❏	❏	❏	❏

Questionnaire

	Strongly disagree	Disagree	Neutral	Agree	Strongly agree
9 We look for a common language to help understanding	❑	❑	❑	❑	❑
10 We make sure our values are clear from the outset	❑	❑	❑	❑	❑
11 A small management group makes the major decisions	❑	❑	❑	❑	❑
12 We acknowledge multiple purposes	❑	❑	❑	❑	❑
13 We focus on learning and continuous improvement	❑	❑	❑	❑	❑
14 We compromise to maintain political stability	❑	❑	❑	❑	❑
15 We establish common standards of behaviour in advance	❑	❑	❑	❑	❑
16 We establish protocols for dealing with our differences	❑	❑	❑	❑	❑
17 It is often difficult to make yourself understood	❑	❑	❑	❑	❑
18 Many different views of the partnership are necessary	❑	❑	❑	❑	❑
19 Some differences have to be planned for	❑	❑	❑	❑	❑

Questionnaire

	Strongly disagree	Disagree	Neutral	Agree	Strongly agree
20 We work at maintaining harmony	☐	☐	☐	☐	☐
21 We encourage participation in decision-making processes	☐	☐	☐	☐	☐
22 It is necessary to satisfy many stakeholders before things get done	☐	☐	☐	☐	☐
23 We establish clear rules and structures	☐	☐	☐	☐	☐
24 Power to get things done is in the hands of many stakeholders	☐	☐	☐	☐	☐

Calculate your score for each set of statements, using the following key:

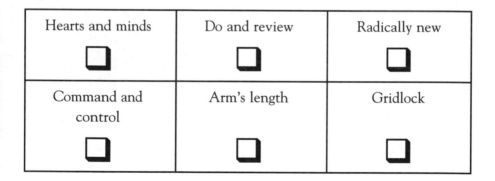

	Statement scores				**Total**
Hearts and minds	= ☐ 1	☐ 2	☐ 10	☐ 20	= ☐
Command and control	= ☐ 6	☐ 11	☐ 15	☐ 23	= ☐
Do and review	= ☐ 3	☐ 7	☐ 13	☐ 21	= ☐
Arm's length	= ☐ 4	☐ 9	☐ 16	☐ 19	= ☐
Radically new	= ☐ 5	☐ 12	☐ 18	☐ 24	= ☐
Gridlock	= ☐ 8	☐ 14	☐ 17	☐ 22	= ☐

Enter your total scores in the appropriate box on the grid. See the descriptions that follow for a summary of the characteristics of each box.

Hearts and minds ☐	Do and review ☐	Radically new ☐
Command and control ☐	Arm's length ☐	Gridlock ☐

Compare your results with a partner's scores on the same task and formulate the five most inportant questions each of you now wants to ask the other.

Partnering grid – summary

Reason for partnering	Hearts and minds	Do and review	Radically new
Promote positive	• Strive for same basic culture (thoughts and feelings) • Shared visions and commitment to common aims • Difference is invisible • Harmony will produce creative outcomes	• Strong process orientation • Changing and complex objectives and constant review • Focus on learning and continuous improvement	• Differences explored for maximum value • Radically new ways of working • Building a shared picture not a shared vision • Involvement of multiple stakeholders • Challenge through dialogue
	Command and control	**Arm's length**	**Gridlock**
Reduce negative	• Strategies to minimize visible differences (formal operations, processes, behaviours) • Negotiated contractual agreements and procedures • Pre-planning to last detail	• Distant relationships with some suspicion • Uniformity by external controls and structures • Acceptance of different objectives and behaviours, but low trust • Clear communication and strict checks on understanding	• Outside forces (regulation, market) constrain partners to reduce negative • Face saving causes lack of momentum • Full recognition of line balance of power causes risk aversion
	Avoid difference	*Tolerate difference*	*Value difference*

View of difference

Appendix C
Partnering objectives assessment

As we discussed in Chapter 3, the fit between objectives, style and operating context is a vital conversation topic for partners. Different partnering approaches fit different objectives. These elements are not fixed and immutable, but vary according to the perceptions and world views of the partners themselves. For this reason it is not possible, or even desirable, to attempt a precise diagnosis of how a specific partnership sees its context. What is possible is to open a conversation between partners that addresses the way the context is seen by all.

The items found in this appendix follow the same special patterns as the grid itself and show the styles most suited to each context. It enables partners to test out fit between their styles (Appendix B) and their view of their context. By adding up the positive responses in all six areas and making sense together of the patterns of similarity and difference, partners can raise their joint awareness of where they 'are'.

Each of the six sets of statements that follow relates to a different partnering context or objective. Scoring the statements and adding up the total score for each of the sets will give you a picture of the most important drivers from the perspective of all the organizations in the partnership.

Think of the core objective of your partnership and tick the statements that best represent your partnering challenge:

Questionnaire

Unitary threat (*command and control*)	Yes	No
Well-understood business environment	☐	☐
Stakeholder influence not an issue	☐	☐
Key knowledge held centrally	☐	☐
Top-down control works well	☐	☐
Clear, accepted source of power	☐	☐
Plentiful resources	☐	☐

Manageable growth (*hearts and minds*)	Yes	No
Growth opportunities on familiar ground	☐	☐
Widely available resources	☐	☐
Little external regulation	☐	☐
Predictable rate of change	☐	☐
Few significant stakeholders	☐	☐
Control is unitary in practice	☐	☐

Sharing risk (*arm's length*)	Yes	No
External barriers to operations	☐	☐
Growing unpredictability	☐	☐
Fiercely competitive environment	☐	☐
Ownership or control divided but clear	☐	☐
Scarce resources	☐	☐
Tight regulation	☐	☐

Exploiting advantage (*do and review*)	Yes	No
Turbulent or unfamiliar environment	☐	☐
Expansion opportunities	☐	☐
Sharing of power, control or ownership	☐	☐
Widening stakeholder community	☐	☐
Strong competition	☐	☐
Accelerating rate of change	☐	☐

Balancing power (*gridlock*)	Yes	No
Strong constraining external forces	☐	☐
Intense political instability	☐	☐
Multiple pressure groups	☐	☐
Resources threatened	☐	☐
Conflicting objectives or purposes	☐	☐
Power widely distributed	☐	☐

Breaking new ground (*radically new*)	Yes	No
Complex, discontinuous change	☐	☐
Knowledge held widely across the whole system	☐	☐

	Yes	No
Ownership and value widely spread	☐	☐
Multiple objectives or purposes	☐	☐
Broad and influential stakeholder community	☐	☐
Steering and control by commitment not force	☐	☐

Scoring

Add up the number of yes scores for each set of statement to determine which section best describes your context. Compare the results to the results of your partnering grid position in Appendix B.

- Is there a good fit?
- Do you have a fully informed view of the context?
- Are there other stakeholders whose views would change the picture significantly?
- Is there a need to review or modify the partnership's objectives?
- Is there a case for trying to adapt your partnering style more fully to the context?

Author biographies

Anne Deering
Vice President, A.T. Kearney, London

Anne Deering has 18 years' experience as a management consultant with A.T. Kearney, working with senior executives to resolve complex business problems. A.T. Kearney is a global management consultancy, with 5,000 employees worldwide.

She is responsible for the creation of Kearney's partnership and leadership intellectual capital, working with both consulting and executive search teams.

Her consulting experience in Europe and North America has been primarily in the areas of partnership development, leadership and team development, organizational learning, organization re-design and strategy.

She is co-author of *The Difference Engine*, a research-based book on partnering approaches and techniques (Gower, 1998). *The Difference Engine* was shortlisted for the business management book of the year award in 1999 by the Institute of Management Consultants.

She is also co-author of *Alpha Leadership: Tools for Business Leaders Who Want More from Life* (Wiley, 2002). Barry Posner, internationally recognized expert in leadership, endorsed *Alpha Leadership* as a book that 'should be read by anyone seriously interested in understanding more about the leadership process'.

Anne holds a BSc in Psychology and a BA (Oxon) in English Language and Literature. She has a Diploma of Management Studies and European Marketing and holds the Diploma of the Chartered Institute of Marketing and the Diploma of the Institute of Linguists (Spanish).

Anne Deering
A.T. Kearney
Lansdowne House
Berkeley Square
London W1X 5DH
United Kingdom
Tel: +44 (0)20 7468 8029
anne.deering@atkearney.com
http:// www.atkearney.com

Anne Murphy
Lancaster University Management School

Anne Murphy is responsible for co-operative partnership development at Lancaster University Management School. She has a background in management learning and extensive international experience as a project manager, designer and facilitator of corporate learning initiatives.

As an Associated Consultant with A.T. Kearney, her work focused on building relationships for research and product development, particularly in the areas of partnerships and networks. She continues this work at Lancaster by developing new relationships at the interface between the academic and business communities. Her role is to foster both local and international connections by bringing together different communities in creative learning and research relationships.

Educated largely in England, she lived in Spain for 14 years and has also spent periods working in the USA, Germany, Holland as well as in the UK. In this peripatetic life, Anne has developed a particular sensitivity to the complex cultural issues of working in partnership, an area in which she has specialized.

She is co-author of *The Difference Engine*, a research-based book on partnering approaches and techniques (Gower, 1998). *The Difference Engine* was shortlisted for the business management book of the year award in 1999 by the Institute of Management Consultants.

Anne holds an MA in Management Learning and a BA (Hons), as well as the Diploma of the Institute of Linguists (Spanish).

Anne Murphy
Entrepreneurship Unit
Lancaster University Management School
Lancaster LA1 4YX
United Kingdom
a.murphy@lancaster.ac.uk
http://www.lums.lancs.ac.uk

Index